Root & Ritual

The Green Witch's Grimoire of Healing, Ritual, and Earth Magic

by Holly Fitzpatrick

REBELLIOUS CROCUS
PRESS
The Alchemy of Ink

Published by
Rebellious Crocus Press
Spokane, WA
ISBN: **979-8-9950510-0-8**
First edition.

For all the women out there
who carry moonlight in their eyes,
love in their hearts,
and curiosity in their minds

This book is for you.
For the seekers who listen to whispers of starlight,
the healers who cradle others with tenderness,
the dreamers who wonder what else is possible,
and the wild souls who know that magic lives in
every stone, every season, every breath,
may these pages be a mirror of your own
brilliance.

You are radiant.
You are powerful.
You are magic.

With Love & Gratitude
Holly

Table of Contents

Awakening to the Green Path: A Witch's Call Home to the Earth

Roots of Magic: The Foundations of Herbal Witchcraft

Guardians of Light: Protective & Purifying Herbs of the Witch's Garden

Hands of the Healer: Restorative Herbs for Body and Spirit

The Heart's Garden: Herbs for Love, Self-Compassion & Connection

Seeds of Gold: Prosperity, Growth & the Magic of Abundance

Sacred Hearth Magic: Herbs of Blessing, Cleansing & Sanctuary

Moonlight & Insight: Herbs for Intuition, Dreams & Second Sight

The Witch's Cauldron: Herbs of Transformation, Release & Rebirth

The Still Grove: Herbs for Balance, Peace & Inner Harmony

Turning the Green Wheel: Seasonal Herb Magic Through the Year

Advanced Herbal Alchemy: The Art of Elemental and Energetic Blending

Earthbound Allies: Working with Stones and Crystals

Root to Sky: A Witch's Farewell & Blessing for the Path Ahead

Additional Rituals

Appendix: Planetary & Elemental Reference Tables

Appendix II: Crystal Correspondence Table

Appendix III: Herbal Safety, Contraindications & Responsible Practice

About the Author

A Welcome to the Green Path

Dear Seeker of the Green Path,

This book is not simply a collection of herbs and spells. It is a conversation between your spirit and the Earth herself.

Within these pages, you will find the wisdom of the plants, the rhythm of the Moon, and the quiet guidance of the Elements. Together, they form a living language, one that speaks through scent, soil, light, and intuition.

As you journey through Root & Ritual, may you read not only with your mind, but with your senses. Let your fingers trace the leaves. Let your breath slow with each ritual. Let your heart open as you write and reflect. Magic does not live only in tools or recipes. It lives in your intention, your awareness, your willingness to listen.

You will learn how to choose herbs by their energy, to blend your own healing brews, to align your practice with the Moon's cycles and the dance of the Elements. You will find rituals, affirmations, and journaling moments designed to bring this magic into your daily life, small sacred acts that remind you that you are nature, too.

Each section of this book holds enough depth to become a book of its own. My intention here is not to overwhelm you, but to open the door and place the tools in your hands. This is an invitation to begin, not a demand to master.

If a particular section speaks to you, follow that pull. Let curiosity guide you deeper. Research. Experiment. Reflect. Trust your intuition to lead you where you are meant to go next. The Green Path is not walked all at once. It unfolds step by step, season by season.

Whether you are new to witchcraft or returning to it, trust that you are exactly where you are meant to be. The Earth has been waiting for your hands, your heart, your remembering.

This book is a beginning, not an ending. More in-depth explorations are already taking root, and I will be releasing expanded works in the future for those who feel called to journey further.

For now, light a candle.
Breathe in the scent of rosemary, of rose, of rain on soil.
Feel the steady pulse of the living Earth beneath your feet. The path unfolds before you, rooted, radiant, alive.

Enjoy the journey
With Love & Gratitude
Holly Fitzpatrick

The History of the Green Witch

The Green Witch is one of the oldest expressions of earth-based wisdom, born from humanity's earliest relationship with the natural world, long before written spells or formal traditions. People learned by watching the land. They observed the way plants grew, healed, nourished, and protected. Those who listened closely, who learned the language of leaves, roots, and seasons, became keepers of this knowledge.

Green Witchcraft did not begin as a title or identity. It was a way of living. These practitioners were herbalists, midwives, gardeners, healers, and caretakers of community health. Their magic lived in kitchens, fields, forests, and hedgerows. It was practical, intimate, and woven into daily survival. To know which plants soothed fever, eased grief, or supported birth was not mystical luxury. It was essential wisdom.

Across cultures, the Green Witch appeared in many forms. In European folk traditions, they were known as wise women, cunning folk, or hedge witches, those who lived at the edge of a village and wild. In other lands, similar figures emerged wherever people lived close to the Earth. Though names differed, the role remained the same. They listened to plants. They honored cycles. They worked with what the land offered.

As organized religion and centralized power expanded, earth-based practitioners became targets of fear and suspicion. Herbal knowledge, once revered, was reframed as dangerous or forbidden. Many Green Witches were persecuted, their practices driven underground. Yet the tradition survived, carried quietly through oral teachings, family remedies, and seasonal customs that endured despite suppression.

The Green Witch's power has never relied on elaborate ritual or hierarchy. It rests in a relationship. The relationship between human and plant, between body and land, between spirit and season. Green Witchcraft recognizes nature as teacher and ally, not a resource to dominate. Every leaf carries medicine. Every season carries instruction.

Unlike ceremonial paths, Green Witchcraft is deeply personal and intuitive. While historical knowledge and folklore are honored, direct experience is equally sacred. A Green Witch learns by tending soil, brewing teas, listening to intuition, and observing how plants respond. Magic arises through attention and presence rather than command.

In modern times, the Green Witch has reemerged as people seek reconnection with the natural world. Climate awareness, herbal medicine, and seasonal living have called this ancient path back into the light. Today's Green Witch may live in a city or countryside, but the practice remains rooted in reverence, sustainability, and deep listening.

To walk the path of the Green Witch is to remember what was never truly lost. It is to step into kinship with the Earth, to honor the wisdom that grows freely, and to reclaim magic as something living, ethical, and profoundly human. The Green Witch does not seek power over nature. She walks beside it, guided by roots, leaves, and the turning Wheel.

Awakening to the Green Path:
A Witch's Call Home to the Earth

"Beneath my feet, the roots remember me.
In every leaf, I find my way home."

Invocation:
The Whisper Beneath the Roots

Close your eyes, and breathe.
Feel the pulse of the Earth beneath you, steady, ancient, alive.
Each heartbeat echoes through soil and stone, through root and
river. This is not the beginning of your journey, but a
remembering.

The Green Path has been calling your name for lifetimes.
 It hums through the rustle of leaves, sings through the rain, and
waits patiently in the herbs that grow wild by your doorstep. To
awaken as a Green Witch is to finally answer that call, to walk
hand in hand with the living Earth, and to honor the sacred
relationship between human and plant, soul and soil.

Here, magic is not performed; it is lived. Every act of care
becomes spellwork, brewing tea, lighting candles, tending
herbs, or whispering gratitude to the garden after rain. You are
both the weaver and the thread, the gardener and the bloom.

The Living Energy of the Green Path

The Green Path is a way of moving through the world with balance, reciprocity, and presence woven into every choice. It teaches that harmony is not imposed, but cultivated through relationship. To walk this path is to slow down enough to notice the living web you are part of, where every action ripples outward and every exchange carries meaning.

At the heart of the Green Path is the understanding that the Earth is not a resource to be extracted, but a relationship to be honored. When you tend the land, the plants, and the cycles that sustain life, you are also tending yourself. The care you offer returns in quiet, steady ways through nourishment, protection, and wisdom earned over time. This is not transactional magic, but mutual devotion.

Every herb you work with carries a living frequency, an energetic signature shaped by soil, sun, rain, and time. Some arrive as protectors, fiery and bold, lending courage and clarity when strength is needed. Others come as healers, soft and nurturing, restoring balance through gentleness and ease. Still others act as teachers, opening inner doorways, guiding dreams, and inviting deeper listening. Each plant meets you where you are, offering what it knows how to give.

Working with herbs is both an art and a dialogue. The Green Witch does not rush this exchange. She listens before she gathers, observes before she blends, and gives thanks before she crafts. She understands that every leaf, root, and flower is a being with its own spirit, purpose, and will. Respect is the first ingredient in every preparation, and relationship is the foundation of every spell.

To walk the Green Path is to return to your natural rhythm. It is a remembering of how to live in harmony with the seasons, the elements, and the lunar tides that shape both land and body. As you align with these cycles, life becomes less about control and more about cooperation. In this living exchange, magic unfolds quietly, steadily, and sustainably, rooted in reverence for all that grows, breathes, and becomes.

The Green Path also teaches the sacred art of reciprocity. For every leaf gathered, a blessing is given. For every root unearthed, gratitude is spoken into the soil. This exchange is subtle yet powerful. It reminds you that you are not separate from the living world but woven into it. The breath you take was once the breath of trees. The nourishment you receive was grown from ancient earth. When you approach your craft with this awareness, even the smallest act becomes a ceremony of belonging.

In walking this path, patience becomes your greatest teacher. Plants do not rush their blooming, nor do they force their unfolding. They grow according to light, season, and unseen intelligence beneath the soil. As you attune yourself to their pace, you begin to release urgency and reclaim trust. Magic ripens in its own time. Intentions planted with care will sprout when conditions are right. The Green Path softens the need to control and strengthens the ability to collaborate with life itself.

There is also humility in this practice. No matter how much knowledge you gather, the Earth remains the greater wisdom. Each season reveals something new. Each plant carries mysteries that cannot be fully mastered, only respected. The Green Witch understands that she is both student and steward. She listens as much as she speaks, observing subtle shifts in wind, soil, and inner knowing. This humility keeps the magic pure and the relationship honest.

Ultimately, the Living Energy of the Green Path is an invitation into intimacy with the natural world. It is a remembering that your body is made of the same elements as root and river, flame and sky. When you walk gently, harvest mindfully, and craft with devotion, you are participating in an ancient rhythm that has never truly been lost. In that rhythm, you discover that magic is not something you perform. It is something you participate in, something that moves through you as naturally as sap through branch and tide through shore.

The Green Path invites you into embodied awareness. It asks you to feel the texture of bark beneath your fingertips, to inhale the sharp sweetness of crushed leaves, to notice how different plants shift your energy simply by their presence. This awareness is not abstract; it is sensory, grounded, alive. When you engage your senses fully, your practice becomes less about memorizing correspondences and more about direct experience. The plants begin to speak in impressions, sensations, and quiet intuitions that no book alone can teach.

And as your relationship with the living world strengthens, so too does your relationship with yourself. The same cycles you witness in the garden unfold within your own spirit. There are seasons of growth and seasons of rest, times of flowering and times of necessary shedding. The Green Path reminds you that nothing is wasted and nothing is permanent. In honoring the cycles of the Earth, you learn to honor your own becoming. Through this sacred mirroring, you discover that tending the land and tending your inner world are, in truth, the very same act.

The Moon as Teacher

The Moon governs not only the tides, but the subtle energies of plants, emotions, and spells.

Each phase carries its own magic, a rhythm that mirrors our own cycles of rest, creation, and release.

New Moon (Beginnings) The dark, fertile soil of intention. Cleanse your altar, drink calming herbs like chamomile, and plant the seeds of new goals.

Waxing Moon (Growth) Energy builds; the sap rises. Work with basil and mint to amplify prosperity, motivation, and action.

Full Moon (Manifestation) The bloom of light and insight. Infuse rose and lavender under moonlight to heighten intuition and self-love.

Waning Moon (Release) Energy recedes, inviting reflection and closure. Burn sage and rosemary to cleanse and clear; compost old herbs to honor endings.

Dark Moon (Rest & Renewal) The still point before rebirth. Meditate with mugwort and myrrh to enter shadow work, rest, and dreaming.

When your herbcraft flows with the Moon's rhythm, your magic becomes a conversation with nature's pulse.

The Elements: Foundations of Green Witchcraft

All herbs embody a blend of the four sacred Elements, the primordial forces of creation that shape the natural world and our own energy.

Earth: The foundation, the root.
Grounding, protection, stability. Found in roots, resins, and woods like vetiver, oak, and patchouli.

Air: The breath, the thought.
Clarity, communication, inspiration. Found in leaves and fragrant herbs like lavender, sage, and lemongrass.

Fire: The spark, the will.
Transformation, action, courage. Found in warming herbs like basil, cinnamon, and rosemary.

Water: The flow, the feeling.
Healing, love, intuition. Found in soft petals and soothing herbs like rose, chamomile, and lemon balm.

As you begin your herbal journey, notice which elements call to you.
Do you crave Earth's grounding or Air's freedom? Fire's spark or Water's flow?
Working with herbs in balance helps harmonize those energies within you.

Preparing to Walk the Path

Before you begin crafting blends, spells, and rituals, take time to create sacred space, both physically and energetically.

Choose Your Space:
A small corner, a windowsill, or a spot in your garden. This becomes your green altar.

Cleanse and Bless:
Sprinkle salt and burn rosemary to purify.
Whisper a blessing like:
"Earth beneath me, Air around me, Fire within me, Water flowing through me, may this space be sacred and true."

Gather Your Tools:
A journal, a mortar and pestle, jars, and a candle.
Let intuition, not perfection, guide your setup.

Invite the Moon:
Work beneath her light whenever possible, or simply imagine her silver energy guiding your craft.

Honor Your Intention:
Before every act of magic, pause. Breathe. Ask:
"What do I wish to create, heal, or release?"

Every act done in awareness becomes part of your spell.

Reflection & Journaling Prompts

Write your answers by candlelight. Let the ink become your first offering to the Earth

What does the Green Path mean to you personally?

____

____

____

____

____

____

Which herbs or plants have always felt special or comforting to you?

____

____

____

____

____

____

____

Reflection & Journaling Prompts

What do you wish to learn, heal, or transform through this practice?

____

____

____

____

____

____

How can you begin infusing daily actions with magical awareness?

____

____

____

____

____

____

Ritual: The First Light

This ritual opens your journey with intention, grounding, and gratitude.

You'll need:
- A white candle
- A small bowl of soil (earth)
- A cup of water (water)
- A sprig of rosemary or basil (fire)
- A feather, incense, or breath (air)

Steps:
Sit comfortably. Breathe deeply.
Light your candle and say:
> *"I awaken to the Green Path.*
> *Root and leaf, flame and flow, guide me home."*

Touch each element in turn, whispering:
- **Earth:** "I am grounded."
- **Air:** "I am clear."
- **Fire:** "I am strong."
- **Water:** "I am open."

Hold the herb to your heart and close your eyes. Feel yourself connecting to the living world.

When you feel ready, extinguish the candle and give thanks.

Keep the herb on your altar as a symbol of your commitment to this path.

Affirmation
"I walk the Green Path with
love and awareness.
The Earth is my teacher,
the Moon my mirror,
and every herb a sacred ally
in my becoming."

Roots of Magic:
The Foundations of Herbal Witchcraft

"Every seed holds a story, every leaf a spell."

Invocation:
Beneath the Soil of Knowing

Magic begins where intention meets nature.
When a witch kneels in the garden, she is both student and
priestess, learning the language of the leaves while weaving
light through her breath.
The Green Witch does not command the Earth; she collaborates
with it.

Each herb you meet is an **ally**, not a tool.
It has a personality, a rhythm, a preferred moonlight.
Some herbs hum softly in the hands, others sing bright in fire.
When you approach them with reverence, they respond,
opening gateways to healing, wisdom, and transformation.

This chapter lays the foundation for that sacred relationship.

The Essence of Herbal Magic

At its core, herbal witchcraft is a living dance between energy and intention. Every plant carries a unique vibration shaped by sun and soil, water and wind, memory and time. When you engage with an herb through ritual, tea, charm, or daily tending, your energy meets theirs, and together you create a resonance capable of subtle but meaningful change. This is how herbal magic shifts reality not through force, but through alignment.

Many witches begin by learning traditional correspondences, calling on rosemary for courage, rose for love, or chamomile to soothe a restless heart. These associations are valuable guides, passed down through generations of practice. Yet they are only the doorway. The deeper magic unfolds when you move beyond memorization and into relationship, allowing your own lived experience with each plant to inform how you work.

Relationship is built through presence. The more time you spend with a plant, smelling its oils, tasting its tea, tending its roots, or watching it grow, the more familiar its energy becomes. Over time, you begin to recognize how it feels in your body and spirit, how it responds to your touch, and how it communicates its gifts. This knowing cannot be learned from a list. It is felt, earned, and remembered.

Through this intimacy, each plant begins to reveal its spirit. Some speak softly, offering comfort and reassurance. Others are direct, protective, or challenging, urging growth and clarity. These impressions become personal teachings, shaping the way you work and deepening your trust in your own intuition. In this way, your practice evolves into a living, breathing grimoire written through experience rather than ink.

A witch does not simply know her herbs; she befriends them. She listens as much as she acts, honors consent as much as outcome, and understands that true power flows from respect and reciprocity. Herbal magic thrives not in control, but in companionship, where plant and practitioner grow wiser together, rooted in mutual care and shared intention.

As your awareness refines, you begin to notice that herbal magic is not confined to formal ritual. It lives in the quiet moments. The way you stir a pot of soup clockwise to call in nourishment. The way you crush dried leaves between your fingers before adding them to a spell, awakening their scent and spirit. The way you pause before harvesting, breathing gratitude into the space between you and the plant. These small gestures are not separate from magic; they are its foundation.

Herbal magic also teaches discernment. Not every plant is meant for every moment, and not every intention requires action. Sometimes the most powerful spell is restraint. A plant may signal that it is not the right time, or that a different ally is better suited to your need. Learning to sense these subtleties strengthens your intuition and cultivates humility. The craft becomes less about commanding energy and more about listening for the current that is already moving.

Over time, this practice reshapes you. You begin to approach life itself as an herbalist approaches a blend, asking what qualities are needed, what energies are excessive, what balance must be restored. The world becomes a garden of correspondences and conversations. In tending your relationships with plants, you also tend your relationship with change, with patience, and with trust. Herbal magic, at its deepest level, is not only about transforming circumstances. It is about transforming the witch who walks the path.

The Moon and the Garden

Just as the tides rise and fall beneath the Moon's glow, so too do plants breathe in rhythm with her light.
By timing your herbcraft to lunar phases, your magic aligns with the natural ebb and flow of energy.

New Moon: The Seed of Intention
A time for cleansing, planting, and quiet creation.
Begin tinctures, cleanses, or new spells. Herbs like sage, basil, and chamomile thrive in this fertile stillness.

Waxing Moon: Growth and Attraction
Energy expands; opportunities bloom.
Work with mint, cinnamon, bay leaf, and rosemary for momentum and motivation.

Full Moon: Power and Illumination
The most potent phase for ritual, manifestation, and clarity.
Harvest herbs for love, intuition, and vitality: rose, jasmine, mugwort, and lavender.

Waning Moon: Release and Reflection

Let go of the old to make space for renewal.

Use cedar, yarrow, wormwood, and lemon peel for cleansing and protection.

Dark Moon: Rest and Renewal

The veil thins; magic turns inward.

Steep mugwort tea for dreamwork or meditate with myrrh and valerian to restore energy.

By aligning your craft with the Moon's rhythm, you're not working against the current; you're flowing with it.

The Elements in Herb Magic

The Elements: Earth, Air, Fire, Water, are the sacred building blocks of all life and the guiding compass for every witch. Each herb holds one or more elemental signatures that influence how it works in both the physical and energetic worlds.

Element	Energy & Intent	Example Herbs	Best Moon Phase
Earth	Grounding, stability, manifestation, protection	Vetiver, Patchouli, Oak, Cedar	Waning → Dark Moon
Fire	Passion, transformation, courage, motivation	Cinnamon, Basil, Rosemary, Ginger	Waxing → Full Moon
Water	Healing, emotion, intuition, love	Rose, Chamomile, Lemon Balm, Blue Lotus	Full → Waning Moon
Air	Clarity, creativity, communication, intellect	Sage, Lavender, Lemongrass, Mint	New → Waxing Moon

To work with an herb elementally, feel its texture, taste, and scent.

Fire herbs are spicy or warm; Water herbs are smooth and floral; Air herbs smell clean and crisp; Earth herbs are musky and grounding.

Practice:

Select one herb from each element.

Breathe it in, meditate, and write how it makes you feel.

Notice whether your body relaxes (Earth), expands (Air),

warms (Fire), or softens (Water).

Reflection & Journaling Prompts

Which of the four Elements do you feel most connected to right now, and which one feels distant?

____

____

____

____

When you imagine your dream apothecary, what herbs and tools do you see?

____

____

____

____

____

____

How do you experience the Moon's energy in your own body or emotions?

____

____

____

____

____

Reflection & Journaling Prompts

What does "balance" mean to you in magical practice?

____

____

____

____

____

____

____

How might you honor the Earth's rhythms in your daily routines?

____

____

____

____

____

____

____

____

Building Your First Magical Apothecary

Creating a witch's herbal apothecary doesn't require hundreds of jars. Start small, and choose herbs you feel drawn to, not just those on a list. Your intuition will know which allies want to work with you.

A beginner's collection might include:
- Rosemary: purification & courage (Fire)
- Rose: self-love & emotional healing (Water)
- Lavender: peace & clarity (Air)
- Chamomile: calm & joy (Water)
- Cinnamon: abundance & action (Fire)
- Sage: cleansing & wisdom (Air)
- Cedar: grounding & ancestral protection (Earth)

Keep them in labeled jars with both their magical and mundane uses. On each Full Moon, hold each jar in your hands and whisper gratitude.

Waxing Moon: Add new herbs to your collection.
Full Moon: Charge them with intention.
Waning Moon: Retire or compost what has grown old or stagnant.
Over time, your apothecary becomes a mirror of your own growth, expanding, refining, and transforming with every lunar cycle.

50 Plant use profiles:

Angelica – Spiritual protection, guidance, and strength in transition.

Anise – Intuition, dream work, clarity, and protection.

Apple – Balance, wisdom, abundance, and ancestral magic.

Ash – Protection, balance, world-tree wisdom, and resilience.

Bay Laurel – Intention setting, manifestation, vision, and success.

Basil – Prosperity, purposeful action, abundance, and protection.

Birch – New beginnings, purification, and fresh starts.

Blackberry Leaf – Protection, boundary setting, and resilience.

Calendula (Marigold) – Protection, warmth, vitality, and joy.

Catnip – Relaxation, joy, attraction, and playful magic.

Cedar – Grounding, purification, ancestral strength, and stability.

Chamomile – Peace, restoration, stress relief, and gentle luck.

Cinnamon – Activation, abundance, passion, and energetic movement.

Clove – Protection, confidence, banishing stagnation, and warmth.

Clover – Luck, abundance, fertility, and shared joy.

Comfrey – Healing, mending, restoration, and Earth connection.

Damiana – Desire, confidence, creativity, and sensual flow.

Dandelion – Release, resilience, wish magic, and personal power.

Elderberry – Immune strength, protection, and deep-rooted wisdom.

Elderflower – Threshold magic, protection, intuition, and blessing.

Fennel – Clarity, confidence, digestion of emotion, and courage.

Frankincense – Spiritual elevation, protection, and clarity.

Hawthorn – Heart magic, protection, ancestral connection, and balance.

Hibiscus – Passion, confidence, beauty, and heart energy.

Hyssop – Cleansing guilt, spiritual renewal, and clarity.

Juniper – Protection, purification, and spiritual clearing.

Lavender – Calm, sleep, gentle protection, and emotional soothing.

Lemon Balm – Joy, emotional lightness, healing the heart, and calm.

Lemongrass – Clearing, renewal, energetic cleansing, and fresh starts.

Linden – Peace, love, emotional safety, and gentle harmony.

Milk Thistle – Cleansing, renewal, boundaries, and resilience.

Mint – Mental clarity, renewal, energy flow, and fresh beginnings.

Mugwort – Dreams, intuition, liminal work, and inner vision.

Myrrh – Ancestral connection, grounding, and sacred space.

Nettle – Strength, nourishment, vitality, and boundary support.

Oak – Strength, endurance, authority, and stability.

Orange Peel – Joy, creativity, success, and solar energy.

Oatstraw – Nervous system support, comfort, and gentle restoration.

Patchouli – Grounding, abundance, sensuality, and rooted desire.

Pine – Renewal, endurance, cleansing, and resilience.

Rose – Heart healing, love magic, emotional balance, and devotion.

Rosemary – Memory, protection, clarity, and energetic cleansing.

Sage – Cleansing, wisdom, boundary setting, and spiritual clarity.

St. John's Wort – Light in darkness, emotional resilience, and protection.

Thyme – Courage, vitality, confidence, and quiet strength.

Valerian – Deep rest, sleep magic, and emotional grounding.

Violet – Emotional healing, humility, spiritual sensitivity, and love.

Willow – Lunar magic, emotional flow, intuition, and release.

Yarrow – Protection, courage, energetic boundaries, and healing.
transformation.

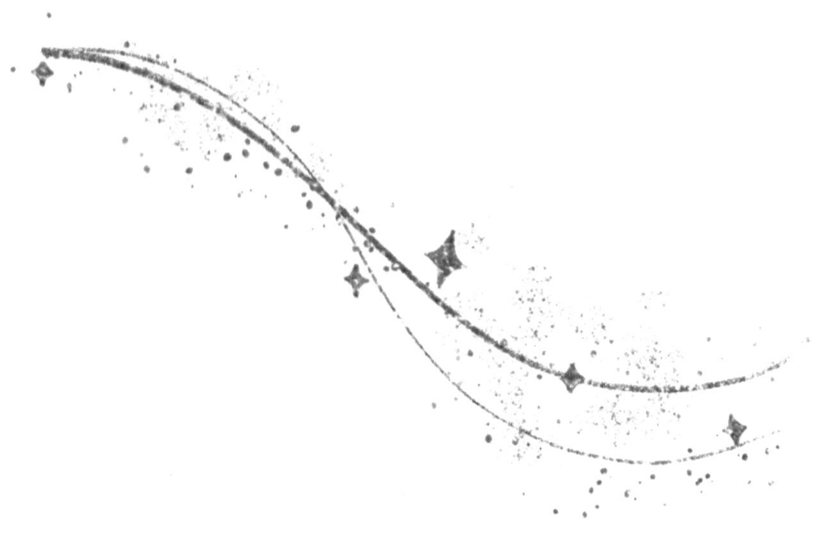

Ritual: Crafting Your First Herb Blend

This simple ritual teaches you to listen to the plants and blend their energy with your own.

You'll need:
- Three dried herbs that call to you (trust intuition)
- A small bowl and spoon
- A candle (white or green)
- A journal

Steps:
- **Light your candle** and take three deep breaths.
- **Hold each herb** in your hand, one at a time. Ask it: "What gift do you offer?"

    Note any sensations, scents, or emotions that arise.
- **Blend the herbs** in the bowl, stirring clockwise to invite harmony.
- **Whisper your intention:**

    "As these herbs blend, so do my body and spirit align with nature's rhythm."
- **Place your hands over the bowl** and imagine moonlight flowing through you into the blend.
- **When finished,** scatter a pinch of your mixture outdoors as an offering, and keep the rest on your altar for one lunar cycle.

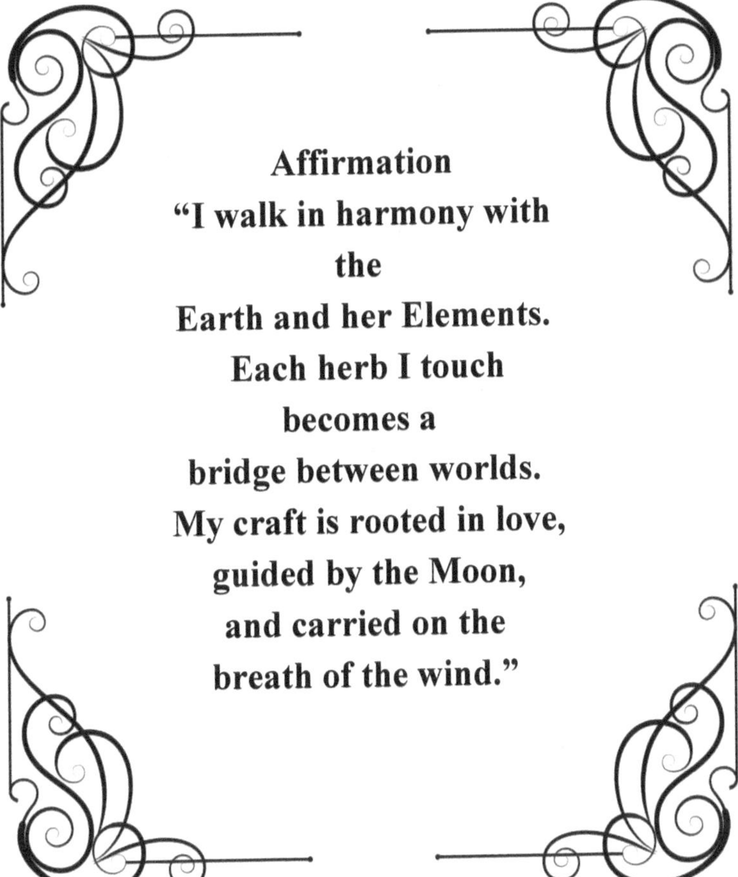

Affirmation
"I walk in harmony with
the
Earth and her Elements.
Each herb I touch
becomes a
bridge between worlds.
My craft is rooted in love,
guided by the Moon,
and carried on the
breath of the wind."

Guardians of Light:
Protective & Purifying Herbs of the Witch's Garden

"Flame and root, shield and smoke, may my circle be clear and strong."

Invocation:
The Keeper's Flame

Every witch carries a flame within, a spark of sacred fire that burns away fear, clears stagnant energy, and lights the way forward.

The herbs of protection are the guardians of that inner fire.

They form the circle that keeps your magic strong, your space peaceful, and your spirit clear.

To cleanse is to make room for clarity.

To protect is to honor your light.

Protection magic is not about building walls; it's about cultivating sovereignty.

When your energy is grounded and luminous, negativity cannot take root.

These herbs are your allies in that work, ancient friends who have stood watch at hearths and doorways for centuries, reminding us that safety is sacred.

The Spirit of Protection

Waning Moon: The most potent time for banishing and cleansing.

Protection magic is not rooted in fear, but in self-respect and awareness. It is the art of maintaining harmony within your energy, your body, and your environment so that you can move through the world with clarity and confidence. True protection is gentle, steady, and preventative rather than reactive.

Protection exists on two interconnected levels: energetic and physical. Energetic protection tends to the unseen, supporting the integrity of your aura and emotional landscape. When your energy is clear and well-boundaried, outside influences have less power to disrupt your inner state. This allows you to remain centered even in challenging environments or conversations.

Energetic protection does not harden or isolate. Instead, it filters. It allows in what nourishes and deflects what drains. Practices such as grounding, breathwork, plant ally connection, and intentional cleansing strengthen this layer naturally, keeping your frequency steady without effort or force.

Physical protection anchors this work in the material world. It includes the care of your living space, the cleanliness of your tools, and the nourishment of your body. Herbal allies that cleanse, fortify, and support resilience act as guardians of vitality, helping to remove stagnation, toxins, and fatigue before imbalance can take root.

When physical environments are clear, energetic work deepens effortlessly. A cleansed space supports focus, intuition, and ritual flow. Likewise, a body that is well-rested and nourished becomes a more stable vessel for magic. The two forms of protection are not separate practices, but reflections of one another.

Protection is also about discernment. Knowing when to rest, when to withdraw, and when to engage is a powerful act of self-preservation. Not every situation requires your energy, and not every invitation needs a response. Choosing where to place your attention is one of the strongest protective practices available.

When both energetic and physical protection are tended with care, you feel anchored rather than guarded. Safety becomes a quiet knowing rather than a constant effort. From this grounded state, clarity emerges, intuition sharpens, and your magic flows with greater depth and confidence.

Protection, when practiced with intention and balance, does not close you off from the world. It allows you to meet it fully, rooted in safety, supported by the Earth, and capable of deeper, truer magic.

Protection also carries an ancestral current. Across cultures and generations, herbs, stones, symbols, and prayers have been used to safeguard homes and hearts. When you practice protection magic, you step into that lineage of guardianship. You are not inventing safety from nothing; you are participating in a timeless remembering that your energy is sacred and worthy of care. This awareness strengthens the work, wrapping it in both personal intention and collective wisdom.

At its highest expression, protection becomes devotion. It is the daily choice to tend your boundaries with kindness, to cleanse your space with gratitude, and to nourish your body as a living altar of spirit. Over time, these small, consistent acts weave an atmosphere of steadiness around you. You no longer cast protection only when something feels wrong. You live in a way that honors balance before imbalance arises. In that steadiness, your magic becomes stronger not because you are shielded from the world, but because you are fully supported within it.

The Elemental Layers of Cleansing

Protection doesn't belong to one element. It's a balance of them all:

- **Earth:** Salt, cedar, black pepper: grounding and sealing energy.
- **Air:** Sage, bay, lavender: clearing mental and energetic clutter.
- **Fire:** Cinnamon, basil, frankincense: burning away stagnation and fear.
- **Water:** Rosewater, chamomile, lemon: soothing emotions and restoring calm.

When performing protection rituals, call upon the elements that feel most aligned. For example, after an argument, you may crave Air and Water herbs for peace. After exhaustion, Fire and Earth herbs to rekindle strength and anchor grounding.

True cleansing moves in layers. You might begin with Air, allowing smoke or scent to lift heavy thoughts from the room. Then call in Fire, igniting transformation and burning away what lingers beneath the surface. Follow with Water to cool and soothe, washing the emotional field clean. Finally, seal with Earth, anchoring the renewed space so the clearing holds steady. Working element by element creates a ritual that feels complete, as though each layer of your being has been tended.

As you deepen your practice, you may find that the elements speak differently depending on the space, the season, or your own inner landscape. A winter cleansing may lean heavily on Fire for warmth and vitality, while a summer ritual may rely on Water to calm intensity. Trust these shifts. Protection is not a rigid formula but a living dialogue between you and the elemental world. When you honor that dialogue, cleansing becomes less about banishing what you fear and more about restoring balance, harmony, and energetic sovereignty.

The Witch's Guardians: Plant Profiles

Rosemary (Rosmarinus officinalis)
- **Element:** Fire
- **Planet:** Sun
- **Lunar Phase:** Full Moon for empowerment, Waning Moon for cleansing
- **Uses:** Protection, purification, remembrance, mental clarity

Rosemary is a witch's first line of defense; fiery, cleansing, and full of solar light.

Burn it as incense to clear stagnant energy, or steep it into an infusion for space cleansing.

Hang sprigs above doorways to ward off discord and invite peace.

Magical tip: Write affirmations of safety or strength on rosemary leaves and burn them to release protective energy into your space.

Cedar (Cedrus spp.)
- **Element:** Earth
- **Planet:** Jupiter
- **Lunar Phase:** Waning Moon
- **Uses:** Grounding, ancestral protection, stability

Cedar's deep scent anchors the spirit. It clears away residual fear and connects you to the steady wisdom of your ancestors. Burn cedar chips to purify, or bundle cedar and sage for a potent smoke cleanse.

Its grounding energy reminds you: you are safe, rooted, and supported by the Earth herself.

Thyme (Thymus vulgaris)

- **Element:** Air
- **Planet:** Venus
- **Lunar Phase:** Waxing Moon for courage
- **Uses:** Courage, confidence, peace of mind

Thyme's gentle energy clears worry and fear from the heart. Brew as a tea before speaking difficult truths or sprinkle in bathwater to cleanse anxiety.

In ancient folklore, warriors carried thyme for bravery. Today, it offers the same spiritual fortitude, helping you stand strong in your truth.

Sage (Salvia officinalis)

- **Element:** Air
- **Planet:** Jupiter
- **Lunar Phase:** Full Moon for purification
- **Uses:** Wisdom, clarity, energetic cleansing

Sage purifies and uplifts as a sacred ally for clearing energetic residue from people, spaces, or tools.

Burn sage with mindfulness, inviting its smoke to rise like prayers of release.

Say aloud:

"As this smoke rises, so does peace.

As the air clears, so does my mind."

Remember: cleansing is an act of love, not destruction.

You are not banishing darkness. You are inviting light.

Bay Leaf (Laurus nobilis)
- **Element:** Fire
- **Planet:** Sun
- **Lunar Phase:** Waxing Moon for strength, Full Moon for success
- **Uses:** Protection, manifestation, mental focus

Bay's radiant energy deflects negativity and strengthens confidence.

Write intentions on a bay leaf and burn it to send your spell into the universe.

Carry dried leaves in your wallet or keep them on your altar for consistent protection and clarity.

Notes:

Add your own

Plant Name:
- **Element:**
- **Planet:**
- **Lunar Phase:**
- **Uses:**

Plant Name:
- **Element:**
- **Planet:**
- **Lunar Phase:**
- **Uses:**

Plant Name:
- **Element:**
- **Planet:**
- **Lunar Phase:**
- **Uses:**

Plant Name:
- **Element:**
- **Planet:**
- **Lunar Phase:**
- **Uses:**

Plant Name:
- **Element:**
- **Planet:**
- **Lunar Phase:**
- **Uses:**

Plant Name:
- **Element:**
- **Planet:**
- **Lunar Phase:**
- **Uses:**

The Energy of Boundaries

Energetic boundaries are the unseen lines that define your personal space and preserve your vitality. They are not walls built in fear, nor barriers meant to isolate you from connection. Instead, boundaries are acts of self-respect. They allow your energy to remain sovereign, clear, and intact as you move through the world, engaging without becoming depleted.

To honor your boundaries is to recognize that your energy is sacred. Just as the land has natural borders - rivers, hedgerows, forests and fields you too are entitled to define where you end and where others begin. Healthy boundaries create clarity, allowing relationships to exist without overreach and exchanges to feel mutual rather than draining. When your energy is protected, you can offer yourself freely and wholeheartedly.

Herbs are powerful allies in boundary work, helping you reinforce these invisible lines through simple, embodied rituals. Burning rosemary before work or social gatherings clears lingering energies and strengthens your sense of presence. Rosemary sharpens awareness and acts as a guardian, creating a protective threshold as you step into shared spaces.

For grounding and steady containment, carry a small sachet of cedar and salt in your bag or pocket. Cedar anchors your energy to the Earth, while salt absorbs and neutralizes what does not belong to you. This quiet charm works continuously, reminding your body and spirit that you are supported, held, and protected wherever you go.

For grounding and steady containment, carry a small sachet of cedar and salt in your bag or pocket. Cedar anchors your energy to the Earth, while salt absorbs and neutralizes what does not belong to you. This quiet charm works continuously, reminding your body and spirit that you are supported, held, and protected wherever you go.

After others have passed through your space, tending to energetic residue is an act of care. A light mist of rosewater and sage restores harmony to your home, clearing what lingers while calling love back into the space. With each of these practices, you offer a gentle declaration to the universe: *I honor my energy, and I keep it sacred.*

Over time, these small rituals become powerful spells, teaching your nervous system that safety, clarity, and sovereignty are your natural state.

Boundaries are strengthened not only through ritual, but through awareness in real time. Notice how your body responds in different environments. A tightening in the chest, fatigue after certain conversations, or a subtle sense of contraction are all messages from your energy field. Listening to these signals without judgment allows you to adjust gently, perhaps stepping outside for air, washing your hands with intention, or placing your feet firmly on the ground to recalibrate. Boundary work is as much about sensing as it is about shielding.

As you practice consistently, your boundaries become less something you "do" and more something you embody. You move with quiet confidence, your presence clear and self-contained. Others feel the steadiness and naturally meet you with greater respect. In this way, energetic boundaries are not defensive structures but luminous edges, defining your sacred space while still allowing connection, compassion, and love to flow freely.

Reflection & Journaling Prompts

How do you currently cleanse or protect your personal energy?

____

____

____

____

What herbs or scents make you feel immediately safe or peaceful?

____

____

____

____

____

What does "sacred space" mean to you, and where do you feel it most strongly?

____

____

____

____

____

Reflection & Journaling Prompts

What situations or people drain your energy, and how might you protect yourself lovingly, not defensively?

____

____

____

____

____

____

____

Imagine your ideal protective boundary. What color, texture, or light does it have?

____

____

____

____

____

____

____

Ritual: The Circle of Light

A simple yet powerful ritual to purify your energy and seal your home in light.

You'll need:
- A white or gold candle
- Dried rosemary, cedar, and bay
- A small bowl of salt (Earth)
- A feather or fan (Air)
- A cup of water (Water)

Steps:

Prepare your space. Open a window. Stand centered and breathe.

Light the candle. Whisper:

"Flame of protection, burn clear and bright.
 Guard this home in love and light."

Sprinkle salt in a circle or along the thresholds, saying:

"Earth below, anchor my peace."

Wave the feather through the herb smoke, letting it drift into corners:

"Air above, carry my prayers of release."

Dip fingers in water and flick droplets gently:

"Water within, cleanse my heart and home."

Stand still as the candle burns.

Visualize golden light expanding from the flame, filling your body, your home, your aura.

When finished, give thanks to the elements and allow the candle to burn safely for a few minutes.

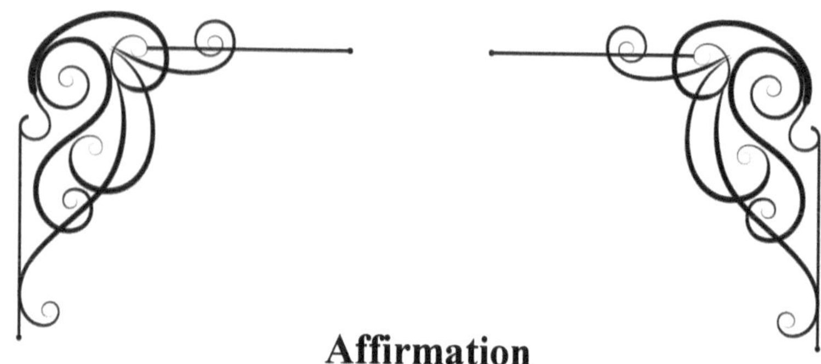

Affirmation

"I am safe, I am clear, I am protected.
Fire burns bright, Earth roots deep,
Air carries calm, Water restores peace.
My light is sovereign, my circle strong."

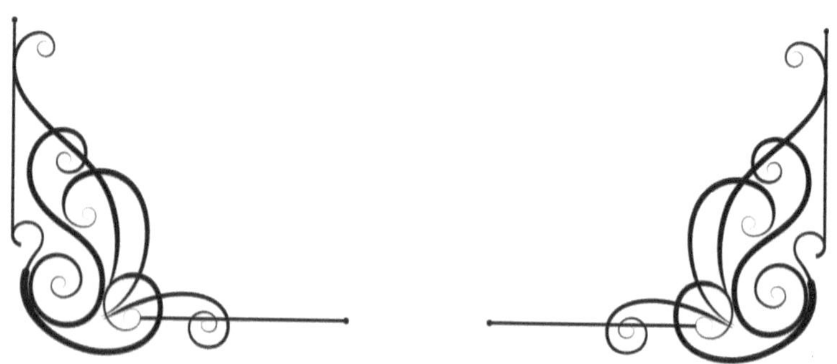

Hands of the Healer:
Restorative Herbs for Body and Spirit

"With gentle hands and open heart, I heal by listening."

Invocation:
The Sacred Work of Mending

Healing is not the pursuit of perfection, but the remembering of your inherent wholeness. It arrives quietly, like steady breath after a storm or the warmth of tea held in tired hands. It does not demand. It reassures. It whispers that you are safe to rest, safe to soften, safe to begin again.

The Green Witch knows that healing begins with presence. To mend is to listen rather than force, to tend rather than rush. Just as a seed cannot be hurried into bloom, your body and spirit unfold toward balance in their own time. Patience and consistency become sacred acts of care.

Herbal medicine reflects this rhythm. Roots fortify slowly, flowers soothe gently, and leaves offer steady support. Through teas, salves, and simple daily rituals, healing becomes a practice of devotion rather than a single event. Each preparation is an affirmation of trust in the body's quiet wisdom.

The hands of the healer are guided by compassion, not control. Healing is not about fixing what is broken, but nurturing what is ready to restore itself. In honoring this sacred work of mending, you remember that wholeness has never truly left you. It has only been waiting for your gentle attention.

The Spirit of Herbal Healing

Every herb that heals the body also soothes the soul. Plants do not separate physical wellness from emotional or spiritual balance. Their medicine moves through the whole being, offering support that is subtle, layered, and deeply intelligent. When you work with herbs, you are not simply addressing symptoms. You are engaging with a living system of care.

Chamomile calms the nervous system while inviting rest and safety. Lemon balm lifts heavy thoughts and restores gentle joy. Calendula soothes irritated skin while strengthening confidence and resilience. These plants offer more than chemical compounds. They carry relationship, memory, and the quiet reassurance of the Earth itself.

Each leaf holds sunlight gathered over time, transformed through soil, rain, and patience. Herbs are the meeting point of Earth and sky, their medicine shaped by seasons, lunar cycles, and elemental balance. When you work with them, you are participating in a dialogue between worlds, one that honors both measurable properties and intuitive knowing.

Herbal healing is as much about presence as preparation. The way you harvest, dry, and store herbs influences their effectiveness. Care taken at each step infuses the medicine with intention, strengthening its ability to support healing. This is why traditional herbalism has always valued mindfulness alongside knowledge.

When you brew a healing tea or prepare an herbal oil, you step into an ancient form of alchemy. Heat transforms water into a carrier of plant wisdom. Time draws out what is needed. Through your hands, raw matter becomes medicine, and care becomes comfort. The process itself is a form of healing.

This work also changes the healer. As you tend herbs and prepare remedies, your awareness deepens. You learn to listen more closely to your body and to the subtle messages of the plants. Over time, confidence grows, not from control, but from trust in the partnership between human and herb.

Herbal healing invites patience. Plants rarely act instantly, but their effects are enduring. They teach that restoration happens through consistency, gentleness, and respect for timing. This approach supports sustainable wellness rather than quick fixes.

To practice herbal healing is to remember that medicine can be loving, slow, and alive. It is an act of devotion to the body, the land, and the wisdom that has always been growing at your feet. When love is infused into medicine, healing becomes more than a result. It becomes a relationship.

Water Element: governs the emotional body; soothing, cooling, nurturing.
Earth Element: rebuilds strength; grounding, stabilizing, restoring. Together, they are the essence of all healing magic.
Waxing Moon: Growth, recovery, vitality.
Full Moon: Wholeness and replenishment.
Waning Moon: Release of pain, grief, or exhaustion.

The Green Healer's Allies

Below are the plants that tend body and spirit alike, your herbal guardians of restoration.

Chamomile (Matricaria chamomilla)
- **Element:** Water
- **Planet:** Sun
- **Lunar Phase:** Full Moon for calm and peace
- **Uses:** Soothing nerves, easing anxiety, inviting restful sleep

Chamomile is sunlight in petal form; gentle, patient, kind. Sip it as tea when your heart feels heavy or your mind won't settle. Add its flowers to ritual baths to release tension and invite serenity.

Spiritually, chamomile teaches the art of soft strength, the ability to stay kind even when the world feels harsh.

Calendula (Calendula officinalis)
- **Element:** Earth
- **Planet:** Sun
- **Lunar Phase:** Waxing Moon for healing and vitality
- **Uses:** Wound healing, regeneration, confidence, joy

Calendula glows like bottled sunlight; a bloom of resilience and renewal. Use its petals in oils and salves for skin healing or in spells to boost self-worth. It reminds the witch that scars are stories of strength, not weakness.

Rose (Rosa spp.)
Element: Water
Planet: Venus
Lunar Phase: Full Moon for love and healing
Uses: Opens the heart, soothes grief, restores self-love
Rose reminds us that love and boundaries coexist.
Add petals to tea or baths for emotional comfort and
forgiveness rituals.
Place dried rosebuds on your altar to represent compassion,
beauty, and the courage to remain open-hearted.

Notes:

Plant Name:
- **Element:**
- **Planet:**
- **Lunar Phase:**
- **Uses:**

Plant Name:
- **Element:**
- **Planet:**
- **Lunar Phase:**
- **Uses:**

Plant Name:
- **Element:**
- **Planet:**
- **Lunar Phase:**
- **Uses:**

Plant Name:
- **Element:**
- **Planet:**
- **Lunar Phase:**
- **Uses:**

Plant Name:
- **Element:**
- **Planet:**
- **Lunar Phase:**
- **Uses:**

Plant Name:
- **Element:**
- **Planet:**
- **Lunar Phase:**
- **Uses:**

Herbal Healing in Practice

To heal with herbs is to step into a relationship with the living world and align yourself with the quiet rhythm of the plants. Herbal healing is not something done to the body, but something entered into with respect and patience. Each leaf, root, and flower carries its own wisdom, shaped by sun, soil, water, and time. When you choose to work with herbs, you are choosing to listen as much as you act. You are entering into a dialogue that unfolds slowly, revealing its insights through sensation, subtle shifts, and lived experience.

When you drink an herbal tea, the medicine of the plant becomes part of you on a cellular level. Its compounds move through your bloodstream, supporting organs, calming systems, and encouraging balance where it is needed most. Warmth spreads through the body, often carrying not just biochemical support but emotional reassurance. When you burn herbs, their smoke becomes a messenger, carrying intention, prayer, and release into the air. When you apply a salve, oil, or poultice, touch itself becomes medicine. Every method of use creates a different conversation between you and the plant, engaging distinct layers of body, mind, and spirit.

Preparation is a sacred threshold in this work. Washing leaves, grinding roots, measuring petals, or stirring a simmering infusion invites you into focused awareness. The scent rising from a freshly crushed herb awakens the senses and signals the body that care is present. The sound of water pouring over dried flowers marks the beginning of transformation. In slowing down, you allow your nervous system to shift from urgency to receptivity. Herbal healing thrives in this softened state. Intention does not replace science, but it enhances it, weaving mindfulness into each step so that healing becomes both practical and spiritual.

Plants are not tools to be taken without acknowledgment. They are living allies who offer their gifts freely when approached with respect. Before harvesting, pause and ask permission, whether aloud or in silence. Notice the condition of the plant and its surroundings. Harvest only from abundance. Afterward, offer thanks through word, gesture, water, or compost returned to the soil. This simple practice creates a foundation of reciprocity that honors the spirit of the plant and the land it grows upon. In this exchange, medicine becomes more than chemistry. It becomes relationship.

Ethical herbalism is rooted in care for the Earth. Take only what you need, and never harvest from struggling or endangered populations. Learn to identify plants accurately and source responsibly when wild harvesting is not appropriate. Support small growers, cultivate your own gardens when possible, and remain curious about the ecosystems from which your herbs come. Giving back can be as simple as tending soil, composting plant remains, planting seeds, or sharing knowledge that encourages others to care for the natural world. When the land is honored, its medicine remains strong.

Healing is not a one-directional act. As you prepare remedies, grow herbs, and tend gardens, the plants shape you in return. They teach patience through slow growth. They teach resilience through seasonal change. They teach humility through their quiet endurance. Working with herbs invites you to observe subtle shifts in your body, emotions, and environment. You begin to notice how stress feels before it becomes illness, how fatigue whispers before it demands attention. Over time, this awareness becomes preventive medicine, guiding you gently toward balance before imbalance deepens.

Working with herbs also invites you to trust your intuition alongside traditional knowledge. Sensations, emotions, and personal responses matter. One person's remedy may not serve another in the same way. A tea that soothes one nervous system may feel too cooling for another. Listening to your body and honoring its responses allows herbal healing to become personalized, adaptive, and deeply supportive. Books provide guidance. Experience refines it. Your own body becomes a teacher in the process.

Herbal healing reminds you that restoration often unfolds gradually. A single cup of tea may calm a moment, but sustained care brings deeper shifts. Consistency builds relationship within the body just as it does with the plants. Gentle daily rituals, even simple ones, accumulate into meaningful transformation. In this way, herbal practice becomes a rhythm of devotion rather than a quick remedy.

True herbal healing is a partnership built on respect, responsibility, and gratitude. When you care for the plants with intention and integrity, they respond with gentle strength and steady support. In this shared exchange, healing flows both ways. As you tend the plants, they tend to you, restoring balance not only within the body, but within your relationship to the Earth itself. And in remembering that you belong to this living world, something deeper than symptom relief occurs. You return to wholeness.

Creating Tea Blends for Ritual Work

Drinking the Spell

To drink a ritual tea is to invite the spell into your body.

Unlike incense that rises into air, or oils that rest upon the skin, tea moves inward. It is absorbed. It circulates. It becomes breath, warmth, pulse. Ritual tea is not simply symbolic magic. It is embodied magic.

When you create a tea blend for ritual work, you are crafting an internal charm, a potion of intention carried through water, plant, and heat.

This is sacred work. It is also simple.

The Foundation of Ritual Tea

All ritual teas begin with three components:

Water

Water carries memory and intention. Use fresh, clean water. As it heats, consider what you are awakening. As it pours over herbs, consider what you are releasing.

Herbs

Each plant carries its own spirit and energetic signature. Choose herbs aligned with your intention, not only magically, but practically and safely.

Heat and Time

Transformation requires both. Boiling water opens the plant. Steeping allows the plant to speak.

In ritual tea, patience matters as much as ingredients.

Choosing Herbs with Intention

Begin by asking: What is this tea meant to support?
(Protection, Love, Clarity, Grief, Abundance, Focus, Rest)

Select herbs whose energetic qualities align with your purpose.
For example:
- Chamomile for peace and gentle prosperity
- Rose for love and heart healing
- Lavender for calm and intuitive opening
- Mint for clarity and renewal
- Cinnamon for vitality and manifestation
- Lemon balm for emotional balance
- Ginger for courage and activation

Always ensure herbs are safe for consumption and appropriate
for your body. Magical intention never replaces physical safety.

A simple ritual blend often contains:
- One primary herb (the core intention)
- One supporting herb (harmonizing energy)
- One catalyst herb (movement or activation)

You do not need complexity. Two or three herbs blended
consciously are often more powerful than ten combined
without focus.

Blending as Spellcraft

Before mixing your herbs, pause.

Touch each plant. Offer gratitude. Speak its name aloud.
Acknowledge its purpose in the blend.

As you combine them, stir slowly in a clockwise direction to
build energy, or counterclockwise to release and banish.
Visualize the qualities merging. Imagine color, scent, and
intention weaving together.

Blending herbs is not mechanical. It is alchemical.
The moment you blend with awareness, the tea becomes more
than ingredients. It becomes intention embodied.

Brewing as Ritual

When you prepare the tea, let the act itself become ceremony.
As the water heats, set your intention clearly.
As it pours over the herbs, visualize activation.
As the tea steeps, allow silence.

Cover the cup while it steeps. This keeps not only heat, but
intention contained.

You may whisper affirmations over the cup.
You may place a crystal beside it.
You may breathe slowly and hold the mug in both hands.
Let the steam rise like an offering.

Drinking with Presence

Do not rush ritual tea.

Sip slowly. Notice temperature, flavor, sensation. Imagine the herbs moving through your body, carrying their qualities into your cells.

If the tea is for grounding, feel your feet.
If it is for courage, feel your spine.
If it is for love, feel your chest soften.

Drinking becomes meditation. The spell completes not in the cup, but in your awareness.

Charging and Storing Blends

If preparing a dry blend to use over time, store it in a glass jar. Label it with its intention. Keep it on your altar if appropriate.

Before each use, briefly reawaken the intention by holding the jar and reaffirming its purpose.

Tea blends lose potency over time, both physically and energetically. Create in small batches. Freshness supports vitality.

A Final Note on Respect

Tea magic is gentle magic.

It does not force outcomes. It nourishes alignment. It works best when paired with action, integrity, and grounded awareness.

When you drink ritual tea, you are participating in one of the oldest forms of plant magic known to humanity. It is simple. It is ancient. It is effective.

You are not merely consuming herbs.
You are welcoming their spirit into your own.
And that is powerful.

Ritual Tea Blends

Protection and Grounding Tea

- Rosemary
- Sage
- Ginger

Supports boundaries and energetic clearing.

Heart Healing Tea

- Rose petals
- Chamomile
- Lemon balm

Encourages gentleness and emotional balance.

Clarity and Focus Tea

- Peppermint
- Rosemary
- Lemon peel

Clears mental fog and sharpens awareness.

Abundance and Confidence Tea

- Cinnamon
- Chamomile
- Orange peel

Warms, activates, and attracts opportunity.

Reflection & Journaling Prompts

What does "healing" mean to you beyond the physical?

____

____

____

____

____

Which herbs make you feel emotionally nourished or spiritually grounded?

____

____

____

____

____

What parts of yourself are asking for rest or softness right now?

____

____

____

____

____

Reflection & Journaling Prompts

How do you show compassion to yourself on difficult days?

____

____

____

____

____

____

____

How might you use daily rituals: tea, breathwork, baths, to weave gentle magic into your healing journey?

____

____

____

____

____

____

____

Ritual: The Healing Brew

A ritual for replenishment, peace, and restoration of spirit.

You'll need:

- Chamomile (calm)
- Lemon balm (joy)
- Rose petals (love)
- Honey (sweetness and harmony)
- A candle (white or soft pink)

Steps:

Light your candle. As the flame flickers, breathe deeply and say:

"With every breath, I call myself home."

Boil water and steep your herbs for 5–7 minutes. As they infuse, visualize golden light swirling in your cup.

Add honey and stir clockwise, saying:

"From root to bloom, from Earth to soul, I drink in healing and wholeness."

Sip slowly. Feel the warmth filling your heart, your body softening.

When finished, thank the herbs and pour any remaining tea onto the Earth as an offering.

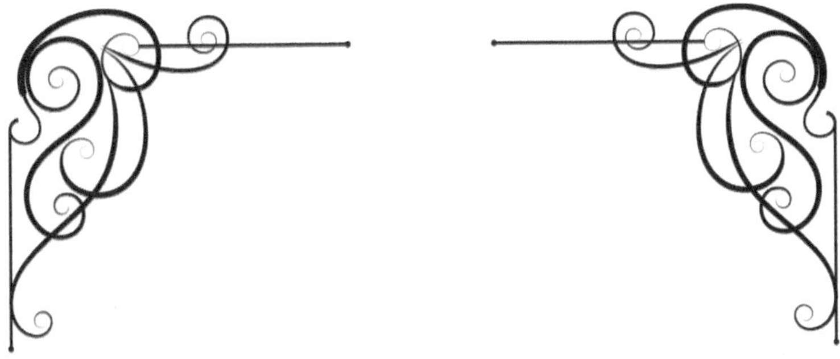

Affirmation
"My body is my temple, my spirit its flame.
I am whole, I am healing, I am harmony.
The Earth restores me, and I rise renewed."

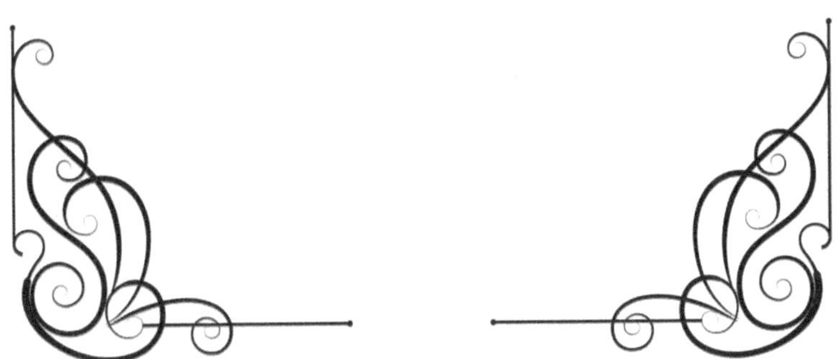

The Heart's Garden: Herbs for Love, Self-Compassion & Connection

"Love is the spell that blooms when we dare to nurture ourselves."

Invocation: The Sacred Flame of the Heart

Love is the language of the Universe. It is the current that connects all beings, the pulse within the soil, the whisper between stars.

The witch who tends her heart tends the world.

Every act of love is an act of magic.

When you offer kindness, you plant seeds of healing.

When you forgive, you water new growth.

When you love yourself, truly, wildly, unapologetically, you become a beacon of light that ripples across lifetimes.

To open the heart is not weakness; it is power refined by grace.

The Spirit of Love Magic

Love magic is not rooted in manipulation, control, or bending another's will. At its core, it is the magic of alignment. It begins within the self, with the cultivation of wholeness, clarity, and self-respect. When love magic is practiced with integrity, it does not reach outward to take. It radiates outward to attract.

True love magic works by refining your inner landscape. As you heal wounds, strengthen boundaries, and honor your own worth, your energetic field shifts. This shift naturally draws relationships and experiences that resonate at the same frequency. What arrives is not forced, but invited.

Love magic is just as much about self-love as it is about connection with others. Rituals of beauty, nourishment, rest, and pleasure are acts of love magic when done with intention. Tending your own heart creates a stable foundation from which healthy, reciprocal relationships can grow.

Herbs, scents, and rituals used in love magic act as allies rather than tools of control. Rose opens the heart without demand. Lavender softens fear and tension. Hawthorn protects the heart while allowing love to flow. These plants support emotional readiness and clarity, not obsession or attachment.

Alignment also requires honesty. Love magic asks you to examine what you truly desire and whether it serves your highest good. Sometimes the magic works not by bringing someone closer, but by creating the clarity needed to release what no longer aligns. This, too, is love.

When your heart is whole, you stop chasing connection and begin embodying it. Love becomes a state of being rather than a goal. From this place, relationships form with greater ease, depth, and mutual respect. Attraction becomes natural, effortless, and sustainable.

Love magic honors free will, timing, and the unfolding path of each soul involved. It recognizes that the deepest magic arises when two people choose one another freely, without enchantment or coercion. Anything less may feel powerful in the moment, but it cannot endure.

To practice love magic with integrity is to trust that what is meant for you will meet you in its own time. By tending your heart, aligning your energy, and honoring consent, you become a magnet for love that is genuine, nourishing, and true.

Herbs of the heart work on multiple layers:
Water Element softens emotional walls and invites vulnerability.
Air Element brings understanding and clarity in communication.
Earth Element nurtures commitment and long-lasting bonds.
Fire Element fuels passion, joy, and creative expression.
Every relationship, including the one with yourself, needs all four to thrive.
Waxing Moon: Attraction and blossoming connection.
Full Moon: Celebration, joy, and passion.
Waning Moon: Releasing grief, healing heartbreak, and forgiveness.

Herbs of the Heart

Rose

- **Element:** Water
- **Planet:** Venus
- **Lunar Phase:** Full Moon
- **Uses:** Self-love, compassion, romance, grief healing

Rose is the queen of the heart; both tender and strong.
Drink rose tea to soften sharp emotions, or sprinkle petals in a bath for comfort and renewal.
Add rose oil to your wrists before meditation or journaling about self-worth.
Each petal whispers: you are worthy of gentleness, including your own.

Jasmine

- **Element:** Fire
- **Planet:** Moon
- **Lunar Phase:** Full Moon or Waxing
- **Uses:** Attraction, sensuality, spiritual connection

Jasmine is moonlight made fragrance.
It awakens sensuality and creative power, teaching that pleasure is sacred.
Use in love spells that celebrate partnership or self-confidence.
Drink jasmine tea before romantic rituals or creative projects to open channels of inspiration.

Hibiscus

- **Element:** Fire
- **Planet:** Venus
- **Lunar Phase:** Full Moon
- **Uses:** Passion, magnetism, beauty, confidence

Hibiscus blooms with boldness, a symbol of self-expression and vibrant life.

Brew into ruby-red tea for confidence before a social event or creative endeavor.

Spiritually, it helps release shame and embrace authenticity.

Apple Blossom

- **Element:** Earth
- **Planet:** Venus
- **Lunar Phase:** Waxing
- **Uses:** Attraction, fertility, nurturing love

Apple blossoms hold the energy of beginnings, gentle, hopeful, sweet.

Use blossoms in charm bags for new relationships or self-renewal.

Cut an apple in half horizontally and you'll find the five-pointed star, a reminder that true love mirrors balance and spirit.

Lavender
- **Element:** Air
- **Planet:** Mercury
- **Lunar Phase:** Full Moon
- **Uses:** Peace, understanding, emotional clarity

Lavender tempers passion with peace.
Burn it or keep sachets nearby to soothe conflict and promote open communication.
It clears the air so the heart can speak its truth.

Notes:

Plant Name:
- **Element:**
- **Planet:**
- **Lunar Phase:**
- **Uses:**

Plant Name:
- **Element:**
- **Planet:**
- **Lunar Phase:**
- **Uses:**

Plant Name:
- **Element:**
- **Planet:**
- **Lunar Phase:**
- **Uses:**

Plant Name:
- **Element:**
- **Planet:**
- **Lunar Phase:**
- **Uses:**

Plant Name:
- **Element:**
- **Planet:**
- **Lunar Phase:**
- **Uses:**

Plant Name:
- **Element:**
- **Planet:**
- **Lunar Phase:**
- **Uses:**

The Alchemy of Love

Love is not confined to romance or partnership; it is the way you move through the world and meet each moment of your life. It lives in the patience you offer yourself during seasons of becoming, in the gentleness with which you tend your wounds, and in the compassion you extend to others even when it would be easier to close your heart. Love is a practice, a choice made again and again to remain open, present, and willing to grow. It is found in the smallest gestures: a softened breath, a kind word spoken inwardly, a willingness to pause instead of react.

To walk the path of the Green Witch is to understand love as a living force, not a fleeting emotion. It is found in the way you speak to the plants as you harvest them, in the reverence you hold for the soil beneath your feet, and in the care you take to honor cycles rather than resist them. This love is steady and rooted, shaped by seasons of growth and rest, abundance and quiet retreat. It does not demand perfection; it asks only for presence. In its presence, even ordinary acts become sacred offerings.

The Earth teaches us that love is cyclical. There are times to bloom and times to pull inward, moments of wild flowering followed by necessary stillness. Just as plants shed their leaves and return again in spring, so too are you allowed to change, soften, and begin anew. Love does not rush this process. It holds space for decay and renewal alike, trusting that nothing is wasted in the great rhythm of becoming. Even heartbreak and disappointment are not failures, but fertile ground where deeper wisdom takes root.

When you practice love in this way, it becomes alchemical. Forgiveness transforms into freedom. Compassion becomes resilience. Self-acceptance turns into quiet power. Through love, pain is composted into wisdom, and past versions of yourself become nourishment for what is yet to grow. This is the sacred exchange between you and the Earth, a mutual tending that shapes both healer and soil. What once felt heavy becomes the rich foundation for future blossoming.

Love also refines your boundaries rather than dissolving them. True love honors truth. It allows you to say no when necessary, to step back when depleted, and to speak clearly without abandoning kindness. In this way, love strengthens your sovereignty rather than weakening it. It becomes the force that protects your energy while keeping your heart open. The Green Witch understands that love and discernment are not opposites, but companions.

To live in alignment with this truth is to remember that love is not something you must earn or chase. It is something you cultivate, moment by moment, through intention, care, and devotion. Like the land itself, you are worthy of tending. You bloom, you rest, you bloom again, and in each cycle, love deepens its roots within you. And as those roots grow stronger, you begin to see that love is not merely something you feel. It is something you embody, something you become, something that quietly transforms everything it touches.

Reflection & Journaling Prompts

What does unconditional love mean to you, in action, not just feeling?

____

____

____

____

How do you show love to yourself on days when you feel least deserving?

____

____

____

____

____

Which relationships nourish your growth, and which drain it?

____

____

____

____

____

Reflection & Journaling Prompts

What does your heart need more of right now, softness, fire, clarity, or roots?

How can you invite more beauty, affection, and creativity into your daily rituals?

Ritual: The Heart's Light

A ritual to awaken self-love, compassion, and emotional harmony.

You'll need:
- A pink or green candle (for love and healing)
- Rose petals
- A few drops of jasmine or rose oil
- A small mirror
- A bowl of water

Steps:
Set the scene. Light your candle and place the mirror beside
Sprinkle rose petals around the flame, whispering:
"As this flame burns bright, so does my heart open to love."
Add oil to the water bowl and swirl gently clockwise. Gaze into the reflection.
Speak aloud:
"I am deserving of love; from others, from the world, and from myself."
Dip your fingertips into the water and touch your heart.
Feel warmth and light expand through your chest.
Close by blowing a kiss toward the candle flame and saying:
"Love flows freely within and around me. So it is.

Let the candle burn safely for a few moments. Dispose of petals outdoors with gratitude

Affirmation
"My heart is a garden of grace.
Love flows through me with ease and joy.
I honor the beauty in myself and in all I meet.
I am both the bloom and the gardener."

Seeds of Gold:
Prosperity, Growth &
the Magic of Abundance

"As I sow, so shall I grow, gratitude turns soil to gold."

Invocation:
The Flow of the Green Current

Abundance is not a thing to chase; it's a rhythm to remember.
It flows like sap through the trees, like breath through your body; rising, falling, expanding, returning.
When you align with that current, everything you need arrives with ease and divine timing.

True prosperity is not only measured in coins but in laughter, peace, and purpose.
It is found in full cupboards and fuller hearts.
The witch who lives in gratitude will always be rich.

Every spell for wealth is really a prayer of trust, a declaration that the Earth provides and that you are ready to receive.

The Spirit of Abundance

Abundance is not limited to money alone. Money is energy, but so are opportunity, time, creativity, joy, and connection. In the Green Witch's world, abundance is measured by flow rather than accumulation. It is the ability to give and receive with ease, to trust that nourishment will arrive when there is space for it to land. A garden overflowing with herbs, a peaceful morning of uninterrupted time, a meaningful conversation that sparks inspiration, these too are wealth.

Fear constricts abundance. Gratitude expands it. When energy is held too tightly, it stagnates. When it is honored and circulated, it multiplies. Abundance magic works by restoring trust in the natural rhythm of exchange, reminding us that the Earth thrives through balance rather than hoarding. The forest does not cling to last season's leaves. The river does not refuse to move forward. Life continues because it flows.

The herbs of prosperity carry solar warmth and fertile vitality. Basil encourages purposeful action and growth. Cinnamon sparks momentum and confidence. Bay seals intention and success. Clover invites shared fortune and mutual benefit. Mint refreshes stagnant energy and stimulates movement. These plants do not promise sudden wealth. They support steady, aligned expansion rooted in clarity and effort.

Working with prosperity herbs is an act of relationship, not demand. When you prepare a tea, charm, oil, or offering with respect, you signal readiness rather than lack. The energy behind the ritual matters as much as the ingredients. Abundance flows more easily when it is welcomed with calm confidence instead of urgency or desperation. You are not begging for increase. You are aligning with it.

Abundance magic begins with care. Care for your living space by clearing clutter and tending what you already own. Order creates room for growth. Care for your resources by using them intentionally and repairing rather than discarding. Care for your body and energy so that you become a vessel capable of holding more. Overflow is difficult to sustain when the foundation is neglected.

Mindset is part of this care. Noticing what is working, acknowledging progress, and celebrating small wins strengthens your energetic foundation. Gratitude is not passive. It is an active alignment with what is present and growing. When you speak appreciation for what you have, you reinforce its presence in your life. When you focus only on what is missing, you amplify scarcity.

True abundance also includes discernment. Not every opportunity is aligned, and not every increase is beneficial. Some forms of gain come at the cost of peace, integrity, or health. Abundance magic teaches you to choose what nourishes rather than overwhelms, what sustains rather than drains. Expansion that compromises your well-being is not prosperity; it is imbalance.

Generosity is another current within abundance. Giving, when done from fullness rather than depletion, keeps energy circulating. Sharing knowledge, offering kindness, and supporting others in their growth, these acts create a web of reciprocity. The Green Witch understands that what is given in alignment often returns in unexpected ways. The form may differ, but the energy remains in motion.

When you honor what you have, you affirm its value. When you tend it with respect, you invite growth. Abundance arrives not as something chased, but as something that recognizes readiness. It gathers where gratitude lives, where trust replaces fear, and where care is practiced consistently. In this way, prosperity becomes not a spell cast once, but a rhythm lived daily, woven into how you think, act, choose, and receive.

Waxing Moon: Plant seeds and set intentions for prosperity.
Full Moon: Manifestation, gratitude, celebration of success.
Waning Moon: Releasing scarcity or fear around money.
Dark Moon: Rest and reflection, resetting your energy flow.

Fire Element: Action, confidence, attraction.
Earth Element: Stability, long-term success, security.
Water Element: Gratitude, emotional harmony with wealth.
Air Element: Ideas, clarity, creative flow.

When all four dance together, you create a sustainable, sacred abundance.

The Green Witch's Wealth Allies

Basil (Ocimum basilicum)
- **Element:** Fire
- **Planet:** Mars
- **Lunar Phase:** Waxing Moon
- **Uses:** Prosperity, protection, success

Basil radiates generosity. It teaches that wealth flows best through gratitude and care.

Keep a basil plant near your door to welcome prosperity and harmony.

Add a few fresh leaves to your meals as you affirm abundance in every bite.

Spell tip:

Sprinkle basil in your wallet or purse with cinnamon and bay for continuous financial flow. *Also see Bay leaf.

Cinnamon (Cinnamomum verum)
- **Element:** Fire
- **Planet:** Sun
- **Lunar Phase:** Full Moon
- **Uses:** Energy, attraction, motivation

Cinnamon is the spark that sets your intentions in motion. It's fast-acting, fiery magic; perfect for when you need to shift momentum or inspire confidence.

Add a pinch of cinnamon to coffee or tea while visualizing your goals blossoming with every sip.

Caution: Its power is strong, use lightly and with clear intention.

Mint (Mentha spp.)

- **Element:** Air
- **Planet:** Mercury
- Lunar Phase: Waxing Moon
- Uses: Success, clarity, renewal, prosperity

Mint refreshes energy and opens the mind to opportunity. It cuts through confusion and reminds you that abundance loves organization and purpose.

Place mint near your workspace or use it in prosperity sachets to attract new ideas and income.

Patchouli (Pogostemon cablin)

- **Element:** Earth
- **Planet:** Saturn
- **Lunar Phase:** Waning Moon for stability
- **Uses:** Grounded wealth, patience, long-term prosperity

Patchouli is slow magic; steady, rich, enduring.

It's the scent of old coins and fertile soil, teaching you that growth takes time.

Use patchouli oil in abundance blends or to anoint candles for business success and resource security.

Bay Leaf (Laurus nobilis)
- **Element:** Fire
- **Planet:** Sun
- **Lunar Phase:** Full Moon
- **Uses:** Victory, protection, success, manifestation

Write your intention or financial goal on a bay leaf and safely burn it under the Full Moon.

The smoke carries your wish to the universe.

Keep a bay leaf in your wallet or altar to maintain the energy of achievement.

Notes:

____

____

____

____

____

____

____

____

____

____

____

____

____

Plant Name:

- **Element:**
- **Planet:**
- **Lunar Phase:**
- **Uses:**

Plant Name:

- **Element:**
- **Planet:**
- **Lunar Phase:**
- **Uses:**

Plant Name:

- **Element:**
- **Planet:**
- **Lunar Phase:**
- **Uses:**

Plant Name:
- **Element:**
- **Planet:**
- **Lunar Phase:**
- **Uses:**

____

____

____

Plant Name:
- **Element:**
- **Planet:**
- **Lunar Phase:**
- **Uses:**

____

____

____

Plant Name:
- **Element:**
- **Planet:**
- **Lunar Phase:**
- **Uses:**

____

____

____

The Energy of Gratitude

Gratitude is the quiet force that sustains true prosperity. It is not performative or forced, but rooted in awareness. When you pause to acknowledge what is already present in your life, you anchor yourself in sufficiency rather than scarcity. Gratitude shifts your inner landscape from longing to belonging, reminding you that you are already held, supported, and nourished by the living world around you. Even in seasons of challenge, there is something steady beneath your feet, something breathing with you, something sustaining you.

To give thanks is to attune yourself to the frequency of "enough." From this place, abundance becomes stable rather than fleeting. When your nervous system relaxes into appreciation, your energy opens and flows with greater ease. Prosperity responds not to grasping, but to grounded receptivity. The universe multiplies what is honored, what is noticed, and what is lovingly received. What you consistently acknowledge becomes stronger in your awareness and, over time, in your lived reality.

Gratitude also refines perception. It trains the mind to see opportunity where it once saw lack, support where it once felt alone. This does not deny hardship. Instead, it widens the lens. You begin to notice small mercies: a conversation that restores hope, a meal that nourishes deeply, a moment of quiet in a busy day. These are not minor gifts. They are threads in the larger tapestry of abundance.

Gratitude is also a form of relationship. When you thank the Earth for her gifts, you acknowledge the sacred exchange between effort and reward, labor and nourishment. The soil offers sustenance, and you offer care. Your work becomes meaningful when it is witnessed with appreciation, transforming daily toil into devotion rather than obligation. In gratitude, even routine tasks become sacred acts of participation in the great cycle of giving and receiving.

This practice can be woven into ordinary moments. Thank the water as you wash your hands. Thank the herbs as you prepare your tea. Thank your body for carrying you through the day. The more frequently you acknowledge support, the more deeply you feel connected to it. Gratitude grounds you in the present moment, where true abundance always resides.

A simple gratitude charm can anchor this energy into your day. At dawn or before beginning your work, speak these words aloud or in your heart:

Thank you, Earth, for the gold in my soil,
for the bread on my table,
for the joy in my toil.

As you recite them, imagine golden light gathering in your chest, warm and steady. See it radiate outward from your heart, touching your home, your work, and your relationships, before returning to you amplified, enriched, and renewed.

Practiced daily, gratitude becomes a living spell. It softens fear, strengthens trust, and invites prosperity to arrive in ways both subtle and profound. When you live in thankfulness, you signal readiness not for excess, but for harmony. And in harmony, blessings grow naturally, like roots reaching deep into fertile ground, steady and sustaining.

Reflection & Journaling Prompts

What does unconditional love mean to you, in action, not just feeling?

____

____

____

____

____

When have you felt truly prosperous, and what made that moment magical?

____

____

____

____

____

Which herbs, colors, or scents make you feel confident and abundant?

____

____

____

____

____

Reflection & Journaling Prompts

How do you balance generosity and self-worth in your life?

Where can you practice more gratitude for the resources you already have?

Ritual: The Bowl of Prosperity and Flow

A sacred charm to invite abundance and gratitude into your home.

You'll need:
- A small green or gold bowl
- Coins or crystals (citrine, pyrite, green aventurine)
- Basil, cinnamon, bay leaves, and mint
- A small candle (green or gold)
- A drop of honey or sugar

Steps:

Cleanse your bowl with smoke or salt. Whisper:

"As I cleanse this vessel, I open the way for golden flow."

Layer your herbs and coins, saying each intention aloud:
- Basil for harmony
- Cinnamon for courage
- Mint for clarity
- Bay for success

Add honey to "sweeten" your energy of receiving.

Light your candle and say:

"Abundance flows to me with ease.

I honor what I have and welcome more in gratitude and peace."

Let the candle burn safely for a while, then snuff it out.

Keep the bowl on your altar or near your workspace.

Refresh herbs monthly, especially at the Waxing Moon.

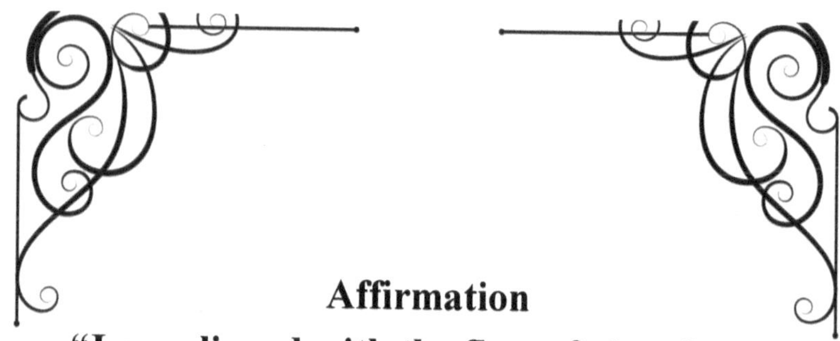

Affirmation
"I am aligned with the flow of abundance.
The Earth supports me,
the Universe provides for me.
Gratitude opens every door,
and prosperity flows freely through my
life."

Sacred Hearth Magic:
Herbs of Blessing, Cleansing & Sanctuary

"My home is my temple, my hearth the flame of peace."

Invocation:
The Flame Within the Home

Every home has a heartbeat; the echo of laughter, the scent of comfort, the warmth of shared meals and whispered dreams. Within these walls, your energy lingers, the imprint of your spirit, your moods, your rituals.

The witch knows that her home is a living being, one that absorbs, reflects, and amplifies the energies within it.
A sacred home is not just tidy; it is tended.

To cleanse is to love your space back into balance.
To bless is to fill it with intention.
To protect it is to claim it as sacred ground.

When the hearth burns bright and the air hums with peace, your magic amplifies naturally.

The Spirit of Home Magic

Home magic begins with the understanding that your living space is not merely shelter, but a living container for your energy. The walls absorb emotion. The floors hold memory. The air carries the subtle imprint of conversations, laughter, grief, and intention. To practice home magic is to recognize that your space responds to you. It reflects your inner state and, in turn, shapes it. When you tend your home with awareness, you are tending your spirit as well.

The Spirit of Home Magic is rooted in presence. It is not about perfection or aesthetic display. It is about intention. A swept floor becomes a clearing ritual. Open windows become invitations for fresh perspective. Lighting a candle at dusk marks the threshold between the outer world and your private sanctuary. These simple acts, performed with mindfulness, transform routine maintenance into sacred practice.

Every home carries an energetic heartbeat. Some spaces feel warm and welcoming. Others feel heavy or unsettled. Home magic invites you to become attuned to these subtle currents. Notice how different rooms feel at different times of day. Notice where clutter gathers or where you naturally gravitate for rest. These patterns offer insight. They reveal where energy flows freely and where it may need gentle redirection.

Cleansing is one of the foundational acts of home magic. Not because your space is flawed, but because energy accumulates. Just as dust settles on shelves, emotional residue settles in corners. Sweeping with intention, diffusing herbs, ringing a bell, or misting water infused with calming plants refreshes the atmosphere. Cleansing restores neutrality. It creates a blank canvas upon which new intentions can be written.

Protection is another layer of home magic. This does not arise from fear, but from care. A bowl of salt near the doorway, protective herbs above a threshold, or a simple blessing spoken as you lock the door creates a boundary of steadiness. Your home becomes a place where your nervous system can soften, where vigilance gives way to rest. In this safety, creativity and healing flourish.

Home magic also includes nourishment. The kitchen, in particular, is a sacred space of transformation. Stirring a pot with gratitude, blessing ingredients before cooking, or placing herbs on a windowsill to dry weaves magic into sustenance. Food prepared with awareness carries a different frequency. It feeds not only the body, but the emotional and energetic layers of those who share it.

Beauty, too, is part of the spell. Fresh flowers on a table, meaningful objects arranged with care, natural light invited in whenever possible. Beauty signals worthiness. It whispers that you deserve comfort and delight. When you curate your space intentionally, you are affirming that your daily life is sacred enough to adorn.

The Spirit of Home Magic reminds you that sanctuary is created, not found. It is cultivated through daily choices to clear, bless, nourish, protect, and beautify your space. Over time, your home becomes more than a structure. It becomes an ally. It holds you through change. It steadies you in uncertainty. It amplifies your rituals and softens your burdens.

Ultimately, home magic is the art of belonging. When your space reflects your values and intentions, you feel anchored. You move through your rooms with ease. You rest more deeply. You create more freely. In tending your home, you declare that your inner world matters. And as you nurture the spirit of your dwelling, it nurtures you in return, quietly and faithfully, day after day.

Home Magic: Cleansing and blessing

Cleansing and blessing your space is not about chasing away negativity; it's about **inviting harmony**.
Herbal smoke, simmer pots, and floor washes are ancient acts of magic disguised as household chores.

As you sweep, you're moving energy.
As you wash, you're blessing.
As you light a candle, you're anchoring warmth into your home's spirit.

Waning Moon: Best for clearing, releasing, and resetting.
Dark Moon: Deep cleansing and ward renewal.
Waxing Moon: Blessings and home growth magic.
Full Moon: Gratitude rituals and light amplification.

Elements of Hearth Magic:
- **Earth:** Stability: salt, cedar, herbs at thresholds.
- **Fire:** Purification: candlelight, warmth, protection.
- **Air:** Clarity: smoke, incense, song, prayer.
- **Water:** Peace: cleansing sprays, baths, emotional calm.

When all four elements are honored, the home hums like a balanced altar.

The Witch's Herbs for Home and Hearth

Rosemary (Rosmarinus officinalis)
- **Element:** Fire
- **Planet:** Sun
- **Lunar Phase:** Waning Moon or Full Moon
- **Uses:** Purification, clarity, protection, uplifting energy

Rosemary clears stale energy and strengthens spiritual boundaries.

Hang dried sprigs above doors or windows to welcom in peace and ward negativity.

Simmer in water with lemon and bay for a simple yet powerful cleansing potion.

Mantra: *"Where rosemary grows, peace follows."*

Cedar (Cedrus spp.)
- **Element:** Earth
- **Planet:** Jupiter
- **Lunar Phase:** Waning Moon
- **Uses:** Protection, ancestral grounding, home stability

Cedar carries the ancient energy of the forest, strong, wise, and deeply rooted.

Burn cedar chips for energetic protection or bundle them with rosemary and sage for a potent cleansing wand.

Its grounding aroma helps a space feel safe and sacred.

Thyme (Thymus vulgaris)
- **Element:** Air
- **Planet:** Venus
- **Lunar Phase:** Waxing Moon
- **Uses:** Courage, harmony, clearing emotional residue

Thyme brightens the energy of any home.
Sprinkle dried thyme on floors before sweeping to remove stagnant vibrations, or add to bathwater for energetic cleansing.
It restores courage and confidence after emotional conflict.

Bay Leaf (Laurus nobilis)
- **Element:** Fire
- **Planet:** Sun
- **Lunar Phase: Full Moon**
- **Uses:** Manifestation, purification, success

Keep bay leaves in kitchen drawers or cupboards to maintain a sense of abundance and protection.
Write wishes or affirmations on them and burn safely to seal intentions into your home.

Salt (Mineral)

- **Element:** Earth
- **Planet:** Moon
- **Lunar Phase:** New or Dark Moon
- **Uses:** Grounding, cleansing, sealing sacred space

Salt is pure Earth, ancient, potent, protective.
Sprinkle it along thresholds, windowsills, or mix with herbs to absorb dense or chaotic energy.
After cleansing, sweep it away or dissolve in water and pour it outdoors or down a drain to release what has been cleared.

Notes:

Plant Name:

- **Element:**
- **Planet:**
- **Lunar Phase:**
- **Uses:**

Plant Name:

- **Element:**
- **Planet:**
- **Lunar Phase:**
- **Uses:**

Plant Name:

- **Element:**
- **Planet:**
- **Lunar Phase:**
- **Uses:**

Plant Name:
- **Element:**
- **Planet:**
- **Lunar Phase:**
- **Uses:**

____

____

____

Plant Name:
- **Element:**
- **Planet:**
- **Lunar Phase:**
- **Uses:**

____

____

____

Plant Name:
- **Element:**
- **Planet:**
- **Lunar Phase:**
- **Uses:**

____

____

____

Hearth Blessing Magic

The hearth is the energetic heart of the home. It may be a literal place, such as a fireplace, stove, or kitchen counter, or it may exist symbolically as the space where warmth, nourishment, and presence naturally gather. Wherever meals are prepared, candles are lit, or loved ones linger, the hearth lives. It is the anchor point of comfort, safety, and belonging.

To bless your hearth is to tend the spirit of your home. This does not require elaborate ritual or grand ceremony, only consistency and intention. A simple daily practice can be profoundly powerful. Each morning, light a candle at your hearth and pause for a breath. As the flame steadies, speak these words aloud or quietly within:

From this flame, peace spreads through every room.
My home is sacred, my spirit is safe.

Allow the flame to witness your intention. In time, this ritual teaches your space to hold calm, protection, and warmth, even on the busiest or most difficult days.

For a more sensory blessing, prepare a hearth simmer pot. Combine cinnamon sticks for warmth and prosperity, orange peel for joy and vitality, rosemary for protection, and clove for grounding and spiritual strength. As the water warms and the aroma fills your home, imagine the air becoming infused with harmony and care. Let the scent move through each room, carrying your intention into the walls, the floors, and the quiet corners of your space.

Lunar timing can deepen hearth magic further. Full Moon hearth rituals amplify joy, gratitude, and togetherness, making them ideal for blessing new beginnings, celebrating milestones, or restoring emotional warmth. Waning Moon hearth rituals are perfect for clearing lingering stress, releasing stagnant energy, and gently resetting the emotional tone of the home. In both phases, the hearth acts as a living altar, reflecting the cycles of rest and renewal that shape both home and heart.

Through these small acts, your home becomes more than a shelter. It becomes a sanctuary. Hearth magic reminds you that peace is cultivated, safety is intentional, and warmth is something you are allowed to create and receive. As you tend your hearth, you tend yourself, weaving protection, comfort, and love into the daily rhythm of your life.

Reflection & Journaling Prompts

What emotions currently dwell in your home's energy?

How do you want your space to feel: calm, inspired, nurturing, vibrant?

Which herbs or scents make your home feel alive?

Reflection & Journaling Prompts

What daily actions could you reframe as magical, sweeping, lighting candles, cooking?

How can you make your home an altar to peace?

Ritual: The Blessing of the Hearth

You'll need:
- A small bowl of salt (Earth)
- A sprig of rosemary or cedar (Fire)
- A cup of water (Water)
- A feather or incense smoke (Air)
- A candle (center of your altar or table)

Steps:
Begin with breath. Feel the stillness of your home.
Light your candle and say:
"Light of protection, flame of peace,
Bless this space, let worry cease."

Sprinkle salt around your main room, focusing on corners and thresholds.
Waft smoke or a feather through the air, envisioning stagnant energy leaving with every swirl.
Flick water droplets gently around your home, saying:
"Water of healing, flow through this space,
Leaving harmony in your grace."

Stand before the candle, place your hand over your heart, and declare:
"My home is sacred. My heart is its hearth.
Love lives here."

Let the candle burn for a while before extinguishing.

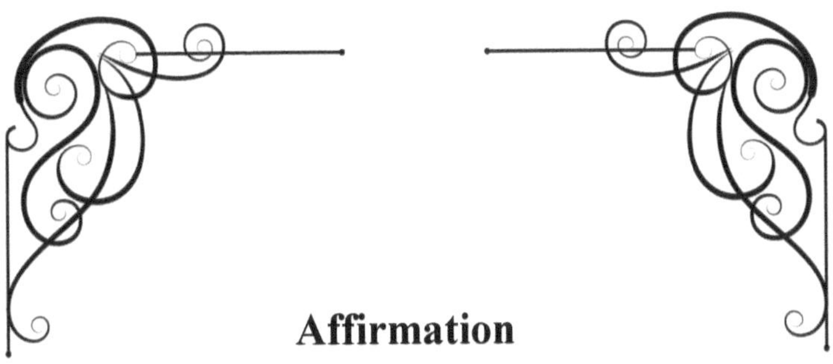

Affirmation
"My home is a sanctuary
of light and love.
Every corner hums with peace,
every doorway welcomes joy.
I am protected, grounded, and held."

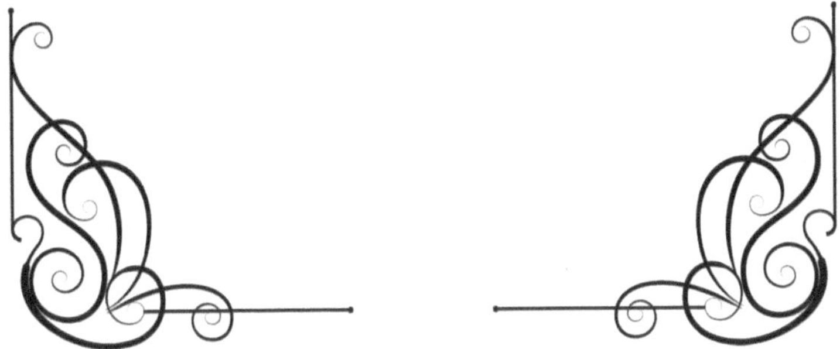

Moonlight & Insight:
Herbs for Intuition, Dreams & Second Sight

"Under moonlight, I remember what my spirit already knows."

Invocation:
Between the Worlds

When the world grows quiet and the stars lean close, the veil between seen and unseen thins.

It's here, in the hush between breaths, that intuition speaks, not in words, but in whispers, symbols, and sensations.

You have always had this gift.
Every dream, déjà vu, and flicker of knowing is a message from your deeper self; the part of you that still remembers the language of energy and spirit.

To work with herbs for intuition is to awaken the senses beyond the five: to trust your inner sight as deeply as your eyes. And to do so safely, you must root before you rise.

The Spirit of Intuitive Magic

Intuition is not a sudden gift granted to a few, but a natural capacity that lives within everyone. Like a muscle, it grows stronger through consistent use, patience, and trust. Intuitive magic asks yIntuition is not a sudden gift granted to a few, but a natural capacity that lives within everyone. Like a muscle, it grows stronger through consistent use, patience, and trust. Intuitive magic asks you to soften rather than strive, to listen rather than demand. Clarity arrives when effort relaxes and awareness widens. It is less about seeking extraordinary visions and more about noticing the quiet wisdom already present beneath your thoughts.

Stillness is the doorway through which intuition speaks. In moments of quiet, the body releases tension and the mind loosens its grip on certainty. From this receptive state, subtle impressions, images, and sensations begin to surface. These messages are rarely loud. They arrive as feelings, shifts, or gentle knowing, and they require presence to be heard. The more you cultivate stillness, the more familiar these subtle currents become.

Intuition often speaks through the body before it reaches the mind. A tightening in the chest, warmth in the belly, goosebumps along the skin, or a sudden sense of ease can all be intuitive signals. Learning to recognize your body's language is a foundational part of intuitive magic. Your nervous system becomes an instrument of perception, translating energy into sensation. When you honor these signals rather than dismiss them, your inner guidance strengthens.

Herbs of intuition support this opening by bridging the conscious and subconscious mind. Plants such as mugwort, blue lotus, and lavender work gently, enhancing perception without overwhelming the senses. They encourage dream recall, symbolic understanding, and emotional insight, helping you interpret the language of intuition with greater clarity. These herbs do not force revelation. Instead, they create conditions of receptivity where insight can rise naturally.

Ritual enhances intuitive development by creating intentional space for listening. A cup of tea prepared with focus, a candle lit before journaling, or a short meditation beneath the night sky signals to your mind and spirit that you are ready to receive. Repetition builds familiarity. The more regularly you enter these spaces, the more easily your awareness shifts into intuitive mode.

Intuitive magic is deeply connected to the Moon and the Water element. The Moon governs cycles, emotion, and inner tides, while Water carries memory, intuition, and psychic flow. Working in alignment with lunar phases strengthens intuitive awareness. The dark moon invites reflection and inner listening. The waxing moon supports growth of insight. The full moon illuminates hidden truths. The waning moon encourages release of confusion and doubt.

Dreams become an important landscape in intuitive practice. Herbs, moonlight, and intentional rest create fertile ground for symbolic messages to emerge. Keeping a dream journal or pausing upon waking to reflect deepens understanding over time, transforming intuition into a reliable guide. Symbols may repeat. Themes may surface. Over weeks and months, patterns reveal themselves, weaving together a personal language of insight.

Trust is essential in this work. Intuition strengthens when honored, even in small ways. Acting on subtle guidance, noticing patterns, and validating inner experiences builds confidence and clarity. Doubt weakens the signal, while gentle acknowledgment amplifies it. Trust does not mean blind belief. It means remaining open long enough to observe how your guidance proves itself through experience.

Intuitive magic also asks for discernment. Not every sensation carries meaning, and not every message requires action. Learning to distinguish between fear, imagination, and genuine intuition is part of the path. Fear often feels urgent and constrictive. Intuition feels steady, even when it guides you toward change. This discernment develops through practice, self-reflection, and emotional honesty.

When intuitive magic is cultivated with patience and respect, it becomes a steady companion rather than an occasional insight. You begin to move through life guided by inner wisdom, attuned to the rhythms of the Moon, the currents of emotion, and the quiet voice that has always known the way. Intuition ceases to feel mystical or distant. It becomes natural, embodied, and woven into your daily choices, a gentle current guiding you home to yourself again and again.

Water: Dreams, emotion, sensitivity, reflection.
Air: Clarity, communication, mental insight.
Full Moon: Heightened intuition and psychic awareness.
Waning & Dark Moons: Shadow integration and protection.
When balanced, these energies allow you to open without overwhelm to sense deeply while staying grounded.

Herbs of Intuition & Psychic Vision

Mugwort (Artemisia vulgaris)
- **Element:** Earth + Air
- **Planet:** Moon
- Lunar Phase: Full or Dark Moon
- Uses: Dreams, divination, protection during spirit work

Mugwort is the Green Witch's dreaming herb: silver-leaved, mysterious, protective.

It enhances intuition, vivid dreams, and psychic awareness.

Burn mugwort before meditation or place it in a dream sachet for lucid dreaming.

Tip: Always pair mugwort with grounding herbs (like cedar or patchouli) to stay centered during deep spiritual work.

Lavender (Lavandula angustifolia)
- **Element:** Air
- **Planet:** Mercury
- **Lunar Phase:** Full Moon
- **Uses:** Clarity, peace, psychic protection, communication

Lavender clears static from the mind so intuition can flow like a calm river.

It strengthens discernment, helping you tell the difference between guidance and fear.

Burn it before divination or anoint your temples with lavender oil before dreamwork.

Blue Lotus (Nymphaea caerulea)
- **Element:** Water
- **Planet:** Moon
- **Lunar Phase:** Full Moon
- **Uses:** Spiritual awakening, lucid dreaming, divine connection

Blue Lotus opens the crown chakra, a flower of insight and grace.

Its gentle euphoria deepens meditation and dream states.

Brew as a light tea or float petals in your ritual bath to enhance intuitive awareness.

Symbolism: Blue Lotus was sacred to ancient Egypt, a bridge between human and divine consciousness.

Damiana (Turnera diffusa)
- **Element:** Fire
- **Planet:** Mars
- **Lunar Phase:** Waxing Moon
- **Uses:** Confidence, creativity, sensual intuition

Damiana reminds us that intuition isn't only mystical, it's embodied.

It connects you to the wisdom of your own body, emotions, and instincts.

Drink it before tarot reading or journaling to open the creative, confident side of your psychic self.

Star Anise (Illicium verum)
- **Element:** Air
- **Planet:** Jupiter
- **Lunar Phase:** Full Moon
- **Uses:** Psychic protection, clarity, dream recall

Star anise looks like the cosmos itself, a star that grounds celestial energy into tangible insight.
Burn it as incense or carry a single pod in your pocket to strengthen spiritual focus and repel confusion.

Notes:

Plant Name:

- **Element:**
- **Planet:**
- **Lunar Phase:**
- **Uses:**

Plant Name:

- **Element:**
- **Planet:**
- **Lunar Phase:**
- **Uses:**

Plant Name:

- **Element:**
- **Planet:**
- **Lunar Phase:**
- **Uses:**

Plant Name:
- **Element:**
- **Planet:**
- **Lunar Phase:**
- **Uses:**

____

____

____

Plant Name:
- **Element:**
- **Planet:**
- **Lunar Phase:**
- **Uses:**

____

____

____

Plant Name:
- **Element:**
- **Planet:**
- **Lunar Phase:**
- **Uses:**

____

____

____

The Moon's Mirror

The Moon is the intuitive witch's greatest teacher, not because she reveals everything, but because she reveals what is ready to be seen. She reminds us that wisdom arrives in phases, that clarity is cyclical, and that no truth demands immediate understanding. Through her gentle light, we learn to trust timing rather than force insight.

As the Moon waxes and wanes, she mirrors the natural rhythm of inner knowing. There are nights of fullness, when awareness feels bright and undeniable, and nights of darkness, when answers are hidden beneath the surface, quietly forming. Both are sacred. The Moon teaches that you do not need to hold constant clarity to be wise. You are allowed to rest within uncertainty and still be guided.

To work with the Moon as a mirror is to practice deep listening. Her changing face reflects your emotional tides, intuitive surges, and moments of retreat. When you feel expansive and inspired, she reminds you to receive. When you feel inward and quiet, she offers permission to soften, reflect, and gather wisdom in the dark. Nothing is lost in these cycles; everything is ripening.

Moon-guided intuition is not loud or urgent. It speaks in symbols, sensations, and subtle shifts of feeling. The Moon invites you to slow down, to notice what stirs beneath logic, and to trust the knowing that arrives without explanation. By observing her phases, you learn when to act, when to wait, and when to simply witness your own becoming.

The Moon's mirror does not demand perfection or constant illumination. It teaches that insight unfolds gently, in its own time. You do not need to see the entire path to take the next step. Like the Moon herself, you are whole in every phase, luminous even when your light is only a whisper in the dark.

Each phase offers a lesson:
New Moon: Quiet your mind and listen. What new intuitive cycles are beginning?
Waxing Moon: Practice trusting your instincts daily.
Full Moon: Heightened visions, journal, scry, or dream.
Waning Moon: Release psychic fatigue; cleanse your aura with rosemary or cedar.

Keep a Dream & Moon Journal beside your bed.
Record intuitive hits, synchronicities, and dreams. Over time, you'll recognize patterns, your soul's personal language of symbols.

Reflection & Journaling Prompts

How does your intuition speak to you through feelings, dreams, or "gut" knowing?

____

____

____

____

____

When have you trusted your intuition and been glad you did?

____

____

____

____

____

What practices help you feel grounded after deep spiritual or emotional work?

____

____

____

____

____

Reflection & Journaling Prompts

Which herbs or scents make you feel most connected to the unseen world?

How can you make space for more quiet listening in your daily life?

Ritual: The Moon's Mirror

This ritual invites clarity and communion with your intuitive self.

You'll need:
- A bowl of water (to act as your mirror)
- A mugwort leaf or sprig
- A few drops of lavender or blue lotus oil
- A white or silver candle

Steps:
Perform during the Full or Waning Moon. Sit near a window where moonlight can touch the water.

Light your candle. Breathe deeply and whisper:
"By leaf and light, by flame and flow,
I open my sight and trust what I know."

Add your herbs and oil to the water. Gaze softly at the reflection, not to see images, but to *feel* impressions.

Ask a question or set an intention for clarity. Let images, colors, or emotions arise naturally.

When finished, thank the Moon and your herbs. Pour the water onto the Earth to ground the energy.

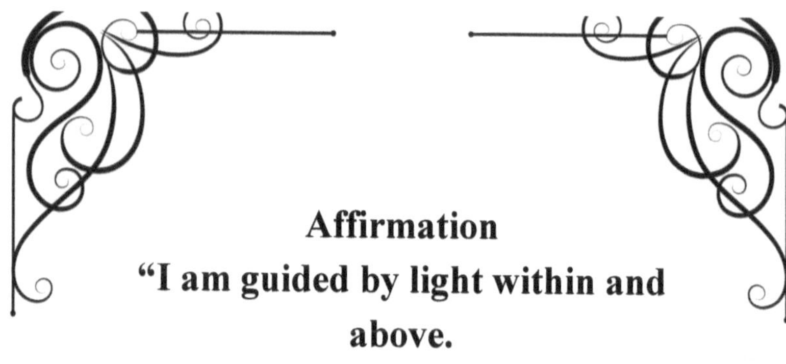

Affirmation
"I am guided by light within and
above.
My sight is clear, my heart discerning.
I trust my intuition as the language of
my soul.
The Moon and I move as one,
luminous,
wise, and free."

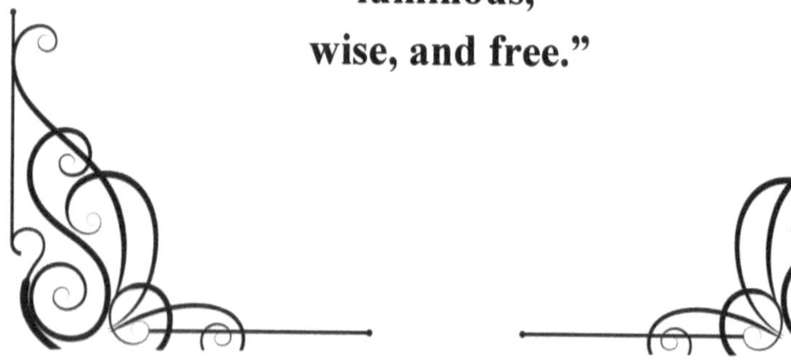

The Witch's Cauldron:
Herbs of Transformation,
Release & Rebirth

"In shadow I stir, in light I rise reborn, renewed, whole."

Invocation:
Descent into the Inner Garden

Every witch must one day descend.

Into the soil of her own soul, into the hidden chambers where old stories sleep.

This descent is not punishment; it is initiation.

For it is in the dark that we remember how to shine.

Transformation does not happen in comfort.

It is the gentle cracking open, the composting of pain into wisdom.

Like the seed that splits to grow, we too must dissolve to become.

The herbs of transformation are the midwives of this sacred unraveling.

They walk with us through grief, shadow, release, and rebirth, whispering, *"Trust the process. The light will find you again."*

The Spirit of Alchemy

Alchemy is the art of turning the ordinary into gold, not just in the physical world, but within. It is the sacred process of transformation that occurs when experience is met with awareness. In the Green Witch's path, gold is not wealth or status, but wisdom refined through living. What begins as confusion becomes insight. What feels heavy becomes meaningful. Alchemy teaches that nothing in your life is wasted when it is consciously tended.

Emotional release, forgiveness, and shadow work are the witch's inner alchemy. These practices require courage, because they ask you to turn toward what is uncomfortable rather than away from it. Shadow work is not about dwelling in darkness, but about illuminating it gently and bringing compassion to the parts of yourself that were hidden or misunderstood. When brought into awareness, these fragments begin to integrate.

To face your truth is to enter the crucible of transformation. Fear often reveals unmet needs. Sorrow deepens empathy. Anger points toward boundaries that require strengthening. Alchemy does not erase emotion. It refines it. It extracts the lesson and the strength hidden within, allowing clarity to rise from what once felt overwhelming.

Forgiveness is one of the most powerful alchemical acts. It does not excuse harm or deny pain. Instead, it releases the hold that past wounds maintain over your present life. In forgiving, you reclaim energy that was bound to resentment or regret. That reclaimed energy becomes fuel for growth, transforming what once burdened you into steady inner strength.

Nature mirrors this process. Compost transforms decay into nourishment. Fire reduces wood to ash, which enriches soil. The alchemical principle is woven into the Earth itself. When you engage in inner work, you participate in this same cycle. Pain becomes compost. Experience becomes wisdom. Even your mistakes feed the soil of future becoming.

Patience is essential in the work of alchemy. Transformation cannot be rushed. The heart, like metal in the forge, reshapes through sustained presence and gentle heat. You may revisit the same lesson more than once. This is not failure, but refinement. Each return strengthens understanding and deepens integration.

The Spirit of Alchemy reminds you that you are not fixed. You are evolving, capable of continual renewal. When you meet your inner landscape with honesty and compassion, you become both the fire and the gold. Transformation is not something that happens to you. It is something you consciously participate in, turning even your darkest moments into luminous wisdom.

Waning Moon: Release, declutter, healing.
Dark Moon: Introspection, shadow work, transformation.
Elements in transformation magic:
Earth: Stability during change.
Fire: Courage and purification.
Water: Emotional release and renewal.
Air: Insight, understanding, and a new perspective

Herbs of Transformation & Shadow Work

Yarrow (Achillea millefolium)
- **Element:** Air + Water
- **Planet:** Venus
- **Lunar Phase:** Waning Moon
- **Uses:** Courage, boundary setting, emotional healing

Yarrow is both warrior and healer.
It teaches discernment, what to keep, what to release.
Add yarrow to ritual baths for strength during change, or burn its dried leaves to banish lingering emotional heaviness.

Lesson of Yarrow: You can open your heart without losing your boundaries.

Dandelion Root (Taraxacum officinale)
- **Element:** Earth
- **Planet:** Jupiter
- **Lunar Phase:** Waning or Dark Moon
- **Uses:** Release, purification, truth-telling.

Dandelion is the humble healer of shadow work.
Its roots draw toxins from the body and emotional debris from the spirit.
Drink roasted dandelion tea while journaling to uncover subconscious patterns and release resentment.
Mantra: "I release the old and trust in renewal."

Myrrh (Commiphora myrrha)
- **Element:** Water + Earth
- **Planet:** Moon
- **Lunar Phase:** Dark Moon
- **Uses:** Spiritual purification, ancestral healing, grief release

Myrrh carries the wisdom of endings.
It cleanses and consecrates, clearing psychic residue and supporting spiritual rebirth.
Burn myrrh resin on charcoal when releasing attachments or honoring ancestors.
Its deep, bittersweet scent says: "Let go. Transformation is love in motion."

Wormwood (Artemisia absinthium)
- **Element:** Fire + Air
- **Planet:** Mars
- **Lunar Phase:** Dark Moon
- **Uses:** Banishing illusions, shadow clarity, courage

Wormwood clears the fog of denial.
It is potent magic: fierce and protective, guiding the witch to see the truth beneath illusion.

Wormwood teaches: "Truth burns, but it also frees."

Valerian (Valeriana officinalis)
- **Element:** Water
- **Planet:** Venus
- **Lunar Phase:** Waning Moon
- **Uses:** Calming the nervous system, emotional release, rest after transformation

Valerian offers peace after intensity.
Drink valerian tea after rituals of release to ease integration and restore calm.
Its earthy energy says, "Rest now. The work is done."

Notes:

Add your own

Plant Name:
- **Element:**
- **Planet:**
- **Lunar Phase:**
- **Uses:**

Plant Name:
- **Element:**
- **Planet:**
- **Lunar Phase:**
- **Uses:**

Plant Name:
- **Element:**
- **Planet:**
- **Lunar Phase:**
- **Uses:**

Plant Name:

- **Element:**
- **Planet:**
- **Lunar Phase:**
- **Uses:**

Plant Name:

- **Element:**
- **Planet:**
- **Lunar Phase:**
- **Uses:**

Plant Name:

- **Element:**
- **Planet:**
- **Lunar Phase:**
- **Uses:**

The Sacred Work of Release

Transformation demands surrender, not as defeat, but as devotion. To release is to trust the unseen currents of magic, to place what no longer serves into the hands of the Earth and allow her to work her quiet alchemy. Letting go is not a loss. It is an offering. It is how space is made for the next becoming.

The witch who understands death as renewal does not fear endings. She knows that decay is sacred, that rot is holy, and that nothing carried away by time is ever truly gone. Every ending is compost, rich and potent, breaking down what once was so that new life may take root. What you release feeds what you are growing.

Release moves first through the body, where old spells were held too tightly. When you cry, you cleanse. Tears are ritual waters, dissolving grief, softening hardened places, and washing stagnant energy back into motion. When you forgive, you unburden your spirit, unbinding cords that once drained your power. Forgiveness is not forgetting; it is reclaiming yourself.

Stillness, too, is a spell of release. In the pause, in the silence, in the sacred nothingness, the nervous system exhales and the soul remembers how to rest. Darkness becomes a womb rather than a void. In that quiet, light does not force its way in, it is invited back gently, when the vessel is ready.

The cauldron is the great symbol of this work. Ancient and eternal, it is the vessel of dissolution and rebirth, where shadow and promise swirl together. In your cauldron, whether wrought of iron or imagination, you place what was, what has ended, and what aches to be transformed. You stir slowly, intentionally, whispering yourself into becoming. What emerges is not the same as what entered. This is witchcraft. This is alchemy. This is the sacred work of release.

Reflection & Journaling Prompts

What in your life or heart feels ready to be released?

____

____

____

____

Which emotions or memories are you still carrying that no longer serve you?

____

____

____

____

What does transformation look like for you: slow growth, sudden change, or cycles?

____

____

____

____

Reflection & Journaling Prompts

How do you care for yourself during emotional release?

____

____

____

____

____

____

____

____

____

What new energy or experience are you inviting in to replace what you release?

____

____

____

____

____

____

____

____

Ritual: The Cauldron of Release

A sacred rite for clearing emotional weight and inviting renewal.

You'll need:

A fireproof bowl or cauldron

A piece of paper and pen

A pinch of yarrow, myrrh, and dandelion root

A black or dark blue candle

Steps:

Set sacred space.

Light your candle and sit before your cauldron.

Take three slow, intentional breaths.

With each exhale, allow your body to soften and your awareness to deepen.

Whisper:

"I enter sacred time. I enter sacred space."

Name what is ending.

On the paper, write what you are ready to release.

This may be habits, grief, fears, patterns, relationships, or old versions of yourself.

Write honestly, without judgment.

Fold the paper toward you, then away from you, sealing the intention.

Add the herbs, one by one.

Place each herb into the cauldron slowly, **speaking its purpose aloud:**

"Yarrow for courage, to face what must be released."

"Dandelion for truth, to loosen what clings too tightly."

"Myrrh for release, to sanctify this ending."

Feel the energy of each plant join the working.

Offer the release to the cauldron.

Place the folded paper into the cauldron atop the herbs. **Say:**

By root and bone, by breath and flame,

I name what ends and loose its claim.

What weighed my spirit, what dimmed my sight,

I give to this transforming night.

Safely burn the paper, allowing flame to consume it fully. As it burns, **say:**

From shadow to soil, from pain to peace,

I honor the end that brings release.

I do not banish, I transform.

I do not resist, I reform.

Witness the alchemy.
Watch the smoke rise.
Visualize your burdens lifting from your body and spirit,
dissolving into light and fertile darkness.

Say softly:
What I release returns as power,
In rightful shape, in destined hour.

Seal the ritual.
Allow the ashes to cool completely.
When ready, bury them beneath a tree or return them to the
Earth, symbolizing renewal and future growth.

Place your hand over your heart and say:
What has ended feeds what comes next.
I am unbound. I am made free.
The cauldron is closed. The spell is set.

Best performed during the **Dark Moon,** when the Earth
herself is releasing, resting, and preparing for rebirth.

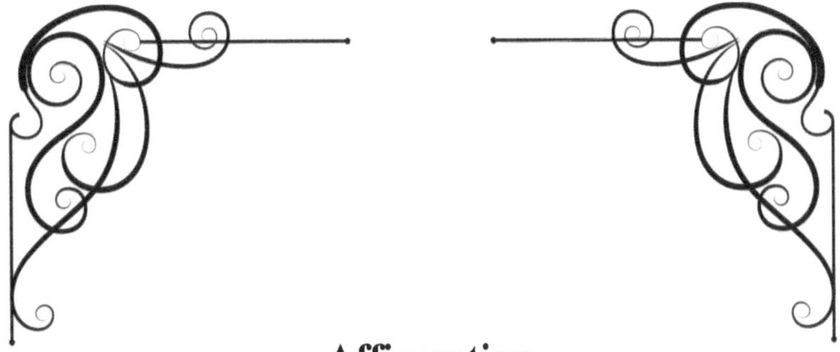

Affirmation

"I honor the dark as sacred ground.
I release what no longer serves my light.
I am not broken; I am becoming.
From shadow I rise, reborn and whole."

The Still Grove:
Herbs for Balance, Peace
& Inner Harmony

"Where wind meets root, I find my calm."

Invocation:
The Quiet Between Breaths

There comes a time in every cycle of magic when the flame softens, the wind slows, and the witch returns to stillness. This is not an ending, nor a beginning, but the sacred pause where power gathers quietly. It is the moment between breaths, between heartbeats, when the body remembers how to listen and the spirit releases the need to strive. In this hush, the world speaks in subtler ways, and wisdom rises from beneath the noise.

This is the space between spells, where intention rests and energy settles into balance. Here, magic is not cast outward, but inward, woven gently through breath, root, and awareness. In the Still Grove, balance is revealed not as something to be achieved, but as a rhythm to be honored. It is the slow dance between light and shadow, giving and receiving, action and rest. To walk this path is to trust that stillness itself is an act of devotion.

Peace is not found in the absence of movement, but in alignment with the flow of life. When you root yourself in the Earth and breathe with her rhythms, even chaos becomes sacred, and uncertainty becomes a teacher rather than a threat. The Still Grove reminds you that calm does not require control. It asks only presence, patience, and the willingness to return to center, again and again, as naturally as breath follows breath.

The Spirit of Balance

Balance is not the absence of extremes, but the ability to move through them with awareness and care. Life carries both joy and sorrow, expansion and contraction, action and rest. The herbs of peace and harmony teach the art of integration, showing us how to hold these opposing currents without being pulled apart by them.

These plants do not erase discomfort or force calm. Instead, they soften sharp edges, allowing tension to unwind naturally. Chamomile, lemon balm, linden, and oatstraw work quietly, restoring equilibrium by supporting the nervous system and inviting the body to remember its own rhythm. Their medicine is subtle, but enduring.

Balance is a living process, not a fixed state. Just as the seasons shift, so does our internal landscape. Herbs of harmony help you respond to change with flexibility rather than resistance. They encourage gentle adaptation, reminding you that steadiness comes from responsiveness, not rigidity.

In Green Witch practice, balance is cultivated through listening. Listening to the body's signals, the emotions beneath reactions, and the subtle guidance of the plants themselves. When you slow down enough to hear these messages, imbalance becomes information rather than failure.

These herbs also teach moderation and pacing. They invite you to rest before exhaustion sets in and to engage before stagnation takes hold. This middle path supports sustainable magic, ensuring that energy is renewed rather than depleted.

Balance extends beyond the self into relationships, work, and environment. A calm internal state influences how you interact with the world around you. When you are centered, your presence becomes stabilizing, and harmony ripples outward naturally.

The spirit of balance honors both light and shadow without judgment. It allows joy to be fully felt without fear of loss and sorrow to be held without becoming overwhelming. In this spaciousness, healing unfolds gently and truthfully.

Through the quiet wisdom of balancing herbs, you are guided back to center again and again. Not because life stops pulling in different directions, but because you learn how to move with it. Balance becomes less about control and more about trust in your ability to return.

Water Element: Emotional flow, acceptance, and gentle release.
Earth Element: Grounding, patience, and restoration.
Air Element: Clarity and calm thought.
Fire Element: Renewed vitality after rest.

Third Quarter Moon: A time of balance, reflection, and restoration.
New Moon: Setting intentions for emotional steadiness.
Full Moon: Offering gratitude for equilibrium and grace.

In this section, you'll meet the herbs that embody serenity, the ones that hush the noise of the mind and restore lightness to the heart.

The Green Witch's Peaceful Allies

Chamomile (Matricaria chamomilla)
- **Element:** Water
- **Planet:** Sun
- **Lunar Phase:** Full Moon
- **Uses:** Tranquility, sleep, easing anxiety

Chamomile soothes both body and soul.
Drink as tea to unwind, or use in a ritual bath before bed.
Sprinkle dried chamomile in your pillow for peaceful dreams.
It reminds us that **rest is not laziness,** it is sacred healing in motion.

Lemon Balm (Melissa officinalis)
- **Element:** Water
- **Planet:** Moon
- **Lunar Phase:** Waning or Full
- **Uses:** Joy, relaxation, emotional clarity

Lemon balm brings sunshine to the spirit.
It's a balm for the heart and mind, light, sweet, and nurturing.
Brew as a daily tonic for mood balance or add to baths when the world feels heavy.

Its magic teaches: Peace is the natural state of the heart when fear is released.

Oatstraw (Avena sativa)
- **Element:** Earth
- **Planet:** Venus
- **Lunar Phase:** Waxing or Full
- **Uses:** Nourishment, resilience, emotional restoration

Oatstraw strengthens from the inside out, calming frazzled nerves and rebuilding energy reserves.

Drink as a nourishing infusion or add to your bath to restore emotional strength.

Oatstraw whispers: You are allowed to rest. The Earth never rushes to bloom.

Lavender (Lavandula angustifolia)
- **Element:** Air
- **Planet:** Mercury
- **Lunar Phase:** Full Moon
- **Uses:** Serenity, clarity, harmony

Lavender bridges the gap between mind and heart. Its scent soothes mental tension and supports honest communication.

Burn lavender incense while journaling or meditating to find inner peace.

Rose (Rosa spp.)
- **Element:** Water
- **Planet:** Venus
- **Lunar Phase:** Full Moon
- **Uses:** Emotional healing, harmony, compassion

Rose reappears here as the heart's stabilizer, helping love and boundaries coexist peacefully.

Add petals to herbal blends for balance between giving and receiving.

Rose is the reminder that peace comes when love and truth stand side by side.

Notes:

Plant Name:
- **Element:**
- **Planet:**
- **Lunar Phase:**
- **Uses:**

Plant Name:
- **Element:**
- **Planet:**
- **Lunar Phase:**
- **Uses:**

Plant Name:
- **Element:**
- **Planet:**
- **Lunar Phase:**
- **Uses:**

Plant Name:

- **Element:**
- **Planet:**
- **Lunar Phase:**
- **Uses:**

Plant Name:

- **Element:**
- **Planet:**
- **Lunar Phase:**
- **Uses:**

Plant Name:

- **Element:**
- **Planet:**
- **Lunar Phase:**
- **Uses:**

The Alchemy of Equilibrium

Balance is not a fixed state to be achieved, but an ongoing conversation between your body and your energy, your spirit and your responsibilities. It shifts as you shift, responding to seasons, circumstances, and inner tides. To seek equilibrium is not to demand perfection, but to remain in relationship with yourself, listening for what is needed in each moment. Some days call for effort and outward focus. Others ask for retreat and restoration. Both are valid. Both are necessary.

When you feel depleted or overwhelmed, the natural world offers a reminder written into every living thing. Return to rhythm. Inhale, exhale. Wax, wane. Rise, rest. These movements are not signs of failure or inconsistency; they are the pulse of life itself. By aligning your pace with these cycles, you allow your nervous system to soften and your energy to recalibrate without force. Rhythm restores what striving exhausts.

Equilibrium also requires honesty. It asks you to acknowledge when you have given too much or withheld too long. It invites you to examine where your time and attention flow, and whether that flow feels nourishing or draining. Sometimes balance means doing less. Sometimes it means engaging more fully. The art lies in discernment, in sensing what will bring harmony rather than further imbalance.

Every imbalance carries a message. Fatigue, irritability, restlessness, and stagnation are not enemies to conquer, but signals asking for attention. They invite you to listen more deeply, to adjust rather than push, and to honor limits before they become wounds. In this way, imbalance becomes a teacher, guiding you back toward wholeness through awareness instead of struggle. What feels uncomfortable may simply be a call to realign.

Herbs act as mirrors in this work of equilibrium. They do not override your body's wisdom; they reveal it. Through taste, scent, and sensation, plants show you where support is needed and where excess can be gently released. A calming herb may quiet overstimulation. A warming one may rekindle sluggish energy. Their medicine works through flow rather than force, encouraging harmony by cooperating with your natural rhythms rather than correcting them.

Water, too, teaches equilibrium. It moves around obstacles instead of battling them. It settles when undisturbed and stirs when influenced by wind or current. When your thoughts feel turbulent, slowing your breath or sipping warm tea can return you to stillness. These small acts are not insignificant. They are adjustments that restore clarity and steadiness from within.

The magic of equilibrium is quiet and consistent. It lives in daily teas, small rituals, intentional pauses, and gentle adjustments made with care. There are no grand gestures required, only devotion to presence and self-respect. Through these small, loving acts, balance becomes not a destination, but a living practice woven into the rhythm of your days. And in practicing this steady return, you discover that equilibrium is less about holding everything perfectly in place and more about trusting your ability to come back to center, again and again.

Reflection & Journaling Prompts

What does balance look and feel like for you?

____

____

____

____

Which parts of your life feel overgrown, and which need more nurturing?

____

____

____

____

____

____

What daily rituals or rhythms help you feel grounded?

____

____

____

____

____

____

Reflection & Journaling Prompts

How can you honor rest as a sacred part of creation?

When was the last time you felt completely at peace? What created that feeling?

Ritual: The Still Grove Ceremony

To restore balance, peace, and calm to the mind, body, and spirit.

You'll need:
- Chamomile, lemon balm, and lavender
- A small bowl of water
- A candle (blue or white)
- A small stone (for grounding, hematite, jasper, or river rock)

Steps:

Light your candle and say:

> *"By flame and flow, by Earth and air,*
> *I call my spirit back to balance fair."*

Add herbs to the bowl of water. Stir clockwise, visualizing the water glowing with golden calm.

Dip your fingertips in the water and anoint your forehead, heart, and hands.

Whisper:

> *"Peace in my thoughts.*
> *Peace in my heart.*
> *Peace in all I touch."*

Hold your stone. Breathe deeply. Imagine roots anchoring you to the Earth.

Sit in silence for several moments. Let the stillness seep into your bones.

Dispose of the herbs respectfully outdoors when finished.

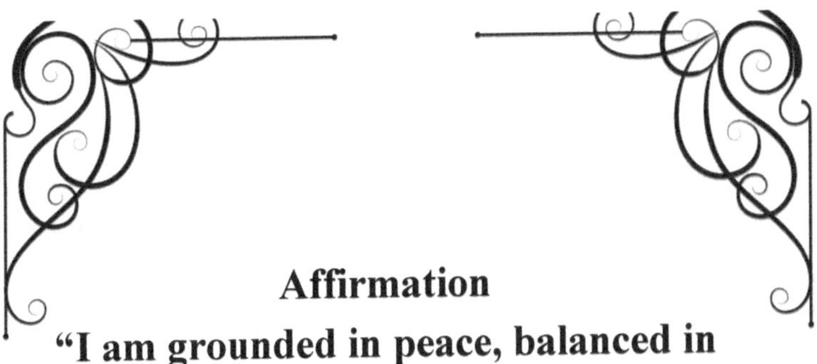

Affirmation
"I am grounded in peace, balanced in
purpose,
and whole in spirit.
My energy flows with the rhythm of the
Earth.
In stillness, I find my strength."

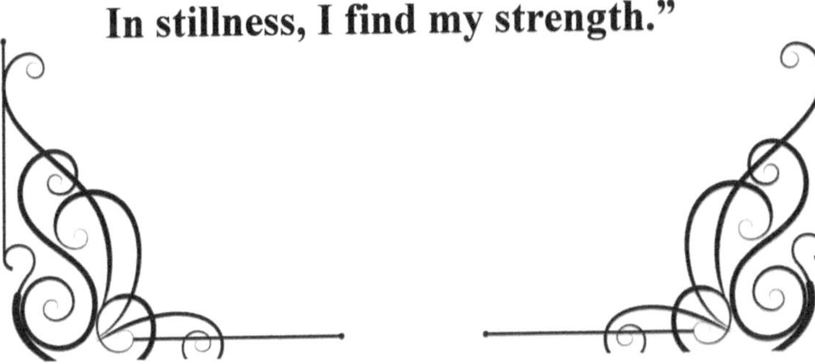

The Still Grove:
Turning the Green Wheel:
Seasonal Herb Magic Through the Year

"The Earth turns, and so do I, in endless bloom and becoming."

Invocation: The Eternal Spiral

The Green Witch walks in rhythm with the turning of the seasons, her spirit attuned to the breath of the Earth, the pulse of the Moon, and the living dance of the Elements. She listens not only with her ears, but with her bones and blood, feeling the subtle shifts of light and shadow as the Wheel moves beneath her feet. In this awareness, time softens, becoming circular rather than linear, a spiral of becoming rather than a line to be chased.

With each turning of the Green Wheel, an invitation is offered: to shed what has completed its purpose, to plant new intentions, to bloom in fullness, and to rest without guilt. These movements are not separate acts, but sacred phases of the same spell, repeating in endless variation. The witch learns to release when the leaves fall, to dream beneath winter soil, to rise with spring's promise, and to expand with summer's abundance, trusting the wisdom of each season in its time.

To live seasonally is to remember that life itself is ritual. Planting and pruning, growing and grounding, celebration and stillness are all woven into the same sacred tapestry. When we honor these cycles through herbal magic, altar tending, and mindful living, we step back into sacred time, the ancient rhythm that hums in every heartbeat, root, and leaf. In this spiral, nothing is rushed and nothing is wasted. The Earth turns, and so do we, held in the quiet magic of endless bloom and becoming.

The Spirit of the Wheel

The Wheel of the Year is an ancient rhythm, turning through eight sacred sabbats that mark the dance between light and dark. These solar festivals reflect the Earth's journey around the Sun, each one revealing a shift in energy, intention, and possibility. As the Wheel turns, it invites us to move with it, honoring cycles of birth, growth, harvest, rest, death, and renewal.

Each sabbat carries its own medicine. Some arrive blazing with fire and abundance, while others whisper softly of rest and release. Along the Wheel, you will encounter moments meant for cleansing and preparation, times for bold action and celebration, seasons for gratitude, and periods for deep inward reflection. The herbs associated with each turning offer guidance and support, mirroring the needs of the land and the body at that time.

To walk the Wheel is to learn the language of timing. Not every season is meant for expansion, just as not every moment calls for rest. The Wheel teaches discernment, patience, and trust, reminding us that growth is not linear. When we honor this rhythm, we release the pressure to be constantly productive and instead embrace a more natural, sustainable way of living and healing.

Working with the Wheel of the Year transforms magic from something occasional into something lived. Ritual becomes woven into daily life through simple acts: brewing seasonal teas, adjusting altar offerings, observing changes in light, or listening to how your body responds to the shifting energies. These small practices anchor you in the present moment and deepen your connection to the natural world.

The Wheel also invites relationship rather than control. Instead of commanding nature, you learn to collaborate with her. You observe, respond, and participate in her unfolding. This approach creates magic that is grounded, ethical, and alive, rooted in respect rather than dominance.

As you move through the sabbats, you may notice how their themes echo within your own life. Beginnings arise when the light returns. Challenges and growth peak under the height of the Sun. Letting go becomes necessary as the days wane. The Wheel reflects not only the seasons of the Earth, but the seasons of the self.

By aligning with the spirit of the Wheel, you step into a practice that honors both ancient wisdom and personal intuition. You become a participant in the great turning, moving in harmony with the land beneath your feet and the cycles within your own heart. This is seasonal magic not as spectacle, but as devotion, lived one turning at a time.

Imbolc (February 1–2) The Quickening Light

Theme: Purification, renewal, and new beginnings.
Moon: New → Waxing
Element: Air
Herbs: Angelica, Bay, Chamomile, Milk Thistle, Rosemary

Imbolc marks the subtle turning of the year, when the light begins to grow though winter still holds the land. It is a threshold moment, neither fully dark nor fully bright, where hope stirs quietly beneath the surface. Traditionally associated with the first signs of lambing and the return of lengthening days, Imbolc honors the spark of life that has survived the cold and is now preparing to rise. The Earth may still appear dormant, yet something beneath the frost is shifting.

This sabbat carries the energy of the first inhale after a long rest. The days stretch slightly longer. The quality of light changes. There is a faint but undeniable quickening. Imbolc teaches that transformation often begins invisibly. Before there is bloom, there is stirring. Before there is action, there is intention. It reminds you to trust subtle beginnings and honor small signs of growth.

This is a season of purification and preparation. Clear stagnant energy from your physical space and your inner world. Open windows if weather allows. Sweep floors with intention. Wash linens. Refresh your altar cloth. Smoke cleansing, herbal baths, and intentional decluttering are especially potent now, helping you release what no longer serves and create space for what is forming. The work of Imbolc is not about rushing forward. It is about readiness.

Air governs this sabbat, bringing clarity of thought, renewal of breath, and inspiration that arrives like a whisper. Focus on mental cleansing as much as physical. Journal freely. Speak affirmations aloud. Practice conscious breathing to release the heaviness of winter. Let your thoughts become lighter. Let your inner dialogue shift from endurance to possibility.

Imbolc invites you to tend the unseen. Like seeds beneath frozen soil, intentions set now do not need to be visible to be alive. This is a season of quiet devotion, whispered prayers, and soft commitments to yourself. What inner fire feels faint but present? What dream has survived the winter of doubt? Nurture it gently. It does not require grand action yet. It requires warmth and belief.

The herbs of Imbolc support cleansing, protection, and gentle awakening. Angelica offers spiritual strength and guidance during transitional moments. Bay carries intention and vision, perfect for writing wishes and burning them safely as offerings. Chamomile soothes and restores after winter's heaviness. Milk thistle supports deep internal cleansing and renewal. Rosemary awakens memory, focus, and inner fire. Together, they create blends suited for purification teas, blessing sachets, floor washes, and renewal rituals.

You may craft a simple Imbolc cleansing infusion by steeping rosemary and chamomile in warm water, then using it to wipe down doorframes and windowsills. As you cleanse, visualize stale energy lifting and new light entering. You may also write intentions on bay leaves and burn them safely, allowing smoke to carry your quiet hopes upward.

Imbolc is the whisper before spring, the moment when the Earth exhales and begins to dream of green. It is a sacred pause to cleanse your altar, refresh your herbs, and prepare your spirit for growth. The light is returning, and so is your capacity to begin again. Even the smallest flame can illuminate a dark room.

Ritual Idea:
Light a white candle and brew chamomile tea. Sit quietly and focus on the flame.

Whisper:
"As light returns, so does my spark."

Journal on what inner fires you wish to rekindle. Write not only what you want to grow, but how you will gently tend it in the weeks ahead. Let this be a promise of warmth to yourself as the year begins to awaken.

Ostara (Spring Equinox, March 20–21)
The Balance of Bloom

Theme: Growth, fertility, harmony, and renewal.
Moon: Waxing → Full
Element: Water
Herbs: Dandelion, Nettle, Mint, Violet, Lemon Balm

Ostara marks the moment of perfect balance, when day and night stand equal and the Earth pauses between dark and light. It is a sacred threshold where potential becomes promise. The long inward journey of winter gives way to outward motion, and the world begins to stretch, soften, and bloom. Life rises visibly now, not just beneath the soil but all around you. Buds swell on branches. Rain nourishes thawed ground. The air itself feels different, alive with movement.

This sabbat teaches that balance is not stillness, but harmony in motion. Light and dark do not cancel each other here; they coexist. Ostara invites you to consider where opposing forces in your life can be integrated rather than resisted. Rest and effort. Giving and receiving. Planning and spontaneity. In honoring both, you create fertile ground for steady growth.

Ostara celebrates fertility in all its forms. Not only the fertility of the land, but of ideas, creativity, relationships, and personal evolution. Seeds planted at this time carry the energy of balance and intention. What you choose to nurture now will grow alongside the returning light, shaped by patience and care. This is an ideal moment to begin projects that require consistency rather than urgency, trusting that small daily tending yields lasting bloom.

Harmony is central to Ostara's magic. This is a time to assess balance within yourself. Where have you given too much or too little? Where does adjustment bring ease? Where can you soften rigidity or strengthen boundaries? Ostara encourages alignment between body, mind, and spirit, inviting gentle recalibration rather than forceful change. Like the equinox itself, you are invited into equilibrium before expansion.

Water governs Ostara, flowing through sap, rain, and blood alike. It supports emotional renewal and physical vitality, making this an ideal time for cleansing rituals that nourish rather than strip away. Think replenishment rather than purging. Drink mineral-rich herbal infusions. Take baths infused with mint or violet. Walk in light rain if possible and allow it to wash away heaviness accumulated during winter's stillness.

The herbs of Ostara are bright, cleansing, and life-giving. Dandelion supports renewal and release, encouraging detoxification and fresh starts. Nettle strengthens and replenishes depleted reserves, fortifying the body with iron-rich vitality. Mint refreshes and stimulates movement, awakening stagnant energy. Violet opens the heart and softens emotional edges, while lemon balm lifts the spirit and encourages gentle joy. Together, they create blends suited for spring tonics, heart-opening teas, and rituals of growth and vitality.

You might create a simple Ostara infusion of nettle, mint, and lemon balm to sip while journaling intentions. As you drink, imagine your roots strengthening and your branches reaching toward light. Let the water element carry your intentions through your body, reminding you that growth is both internal and external.

Ostara invites action, but not urgency. Growth happens naturally when conditions are right. There is no need to force bloom before its time. Trust the process unfolding within you and around you. Balance is the foundation of lasting expansion. From this place of harmony, your efforts become sustainable and your dreams take root with resilience.

Ritual Idea:
Plant seeds or tend seedlings while setting intentions for creativity, health, or new ventures. As your hands press soil around the seeds, say:
"As the Earth awakens, so does my dream."
Water them gently and commit to tending both plant and intention with steady devotion in the weeks to come.

Beltane (April 30–May 1) The Fire of Union

Theme: Passion, love, creativity, and vitality.
Moon: Full
Element: Fire
Herbs: Rose, Jasmine, Hawthorn, Thyme, Clover

Beltane marks the height of spring's fertility, when the land is lush, fragrant, and alive with desire. Blossoms open wide. Bees hum in golden air. The Earth feels abundant and generous. It is a festival of union, celebrating the sacred marriage between Earth and Sky, seed and soil, body and spirit. At Beltane, life does not whisper. It sings, blooms, and burns bright with possibility.

This sabbat honors passion in all its forms. Romantic love, creative fire, physical vitality, and the joy of being fully embodied are sacred expressions of this season. Beltane invites you to say yes to pleasure, to movement, and to the things that make you feel fully alive in your skin. It is a reminder that joy is not frivolous. Joy is life force. When you follow what lights you up, you align yourself with the fertile current of the season.

The Full Moon energy often accompanying Beltane amplifies emotion and magnetism. Desires rise to the surface, asking to be acknowledged rather than hidden. This is a potent time for heart-centered manifestation, especially those intentions rooted in love, connection, and creative expression. What you claim with confidence under this moon carries the warmth of both lunar radiance and earthly fire.

Fire governs Beltane, igniting courage, confidence, and desire. This is a time to act on what has been quietly growing since Ostara. Seeds planted earlier in the season now push toward expression. Whether through art, intimacy, collaboration, or celebration, Beltane encourages boldness tempered by reverence. Fire transforms inspiration into action. It asks you to move, not just dream.

The herbs of Beltane reflect love, vitality, and heart-centered magic. Rose opens the heart and deepens emotional connection, softening fear and strengthening affection. Jasmine awakens sensuality and intuitive awareness, heightening the senses. Hawthorn, sacred to this season, strengthens the heart while honoring sacred boundaries in love. Thyme offers courage and subtle protection, while clover symbolizes abundance, luck, and shared joy. Blended together, these herbs create powerful allies for attraction, celebration, and creative flow.

Beltane is also a time to honor the body as sacred. Movement becomes ritual. Dance becomes prayer. Laughter becomes blessing. When you engage your senses fully, you ground magic into the physical world. The warmth of sunlight on skin, the scent of blooming flowers, the rhythm of music through your feet, these experiences are not separate from spirituality. They are expressions of it.

Yet within the exuberance of Beltane lies wisdom. Fire can warm or consume. Passion can uplift or overwhelm. This sabbat teaches conscious celebration. What you celebrate now becomes what you strengthen. Choose joy that nourishes rather than depletes. Choose connection that honors your spirit. Feed desires that align with your truth, and allow fleeting impulses to pass like sparks into night air.

Beltane reminds you that union begins within. The marriage of your own inner fire and grounded presence creates wholeness. When you honor both desire and discernment, pleasure and purpose, your vitality becomes sustainable. You are not meant to dim your flame. You are meant to tend it wisely.

Ritual Idea:
Create a Beltane incense blend of dried rose petals, thyme, and clover. Light a candle or small fire. Burn the blend safely while dancing, moving, or journaling about what truly brings you alive.
Say:
"As fire and flower entwine, my spirit dances free."

Allow yourself to feel gratitude for your body, your passions, and the creative current flowing through you.

Litha (Summer Solstice, June 20–22)
The Sun at Zenith

Theme: Abundance, vitality, illumination, gratitude.
Moon: Full
Element: Fire + Air
Herbs: Lemon Balm, Thyme, Rosemary, St. John's Wort, Sage

Litha marks the longest day of the year, when the Sun stands at its highest point in the sky and the world is drenched in light. This sabbat honors fullness, visibility, and life in its most expansive expression. The Earth is rich with growth, and the energy of creation feels strong, confident, and alive.

At Litha, we celebrate abundance not as excess, but as presence. This is a moment to acknowledge what has come into bloom through your care and intention. The light of the Sun reveals both blessings and truths, inviting clarity, honesty, and appreciation for the path you are walking. Illumination at Litha is not only external. It shines inward as well.

Fire and Air combine at this turning of the Wheel, blending passion with awareness. Fire fuels vitality and confidence, while Air carries insight, inspiration, and expression. Together, they encourage you to stand fully in your power, speak your truth, and celebrate your place within the living world.

Litha is also a powerful time for harvesting herbs at their peak potency. Plants gathered now are believed to carry heightened solar energy, making them especially effective for protection, vitality, healing, and clarity work throughout the year. Drying, bundling, and storing herbs at Litha becomes an act of future magic, preserving summer's light for darker days.

The herbs of Litha reflect brightness, strength, and purification. Lemon balm lifts the spirit and encourages joy. Thyme offers courage and resilience. Rosemary sharpens memory and focus. St. John's wort supports emotional lightness and protection, while sage clears stagnant energy and honors wisdom. These herbs are well-suited for solar infusions, incense, and blessing rituals.

Gratitude is the heart of Litha. This sabbat asks you to pause and recognize the abundance already present, rather than chasing what is not yet formed. Gratitude anchors joy, making it sustainable rather than fleeting. By honoring what is, you strengthen the flow of what will be.

As the Sun reaches its zenith, it also begins its gradual return toward darkness. Litha gently reminds us that all fullness contains the seed of change. This awareness deepens gratitude and invites you to savor the moment without clinging to it.

Ritual Idea:
Prepare a gratitude potion by steeping lemon balm and thyme in water charged under the Solstice Sun.
As you sip, say: *"Light within, light without, I shine in gratitude and grace."*

Lammas / Lughnasadh (August 1–2)
The First Harvest

Theme: Gratitude, abundance, and manifestation.
Moon: Waning
Element: Earth
Herbs: Basil, Chamomile, Oatstraw, Cinnamon, Bay

Lammas marks the first gathering of the year's harvest, when the early grains are cut and the fruits of long effort become visible. Fields once green and tender now bow heavy with wheat. Gardens overflow with herbs and vegetables. This sabbat honors the moment when intention turns into tangible result. What was planted in hope during spring now shows its shape, revealing both successes and lessons earned through patience and care. It is the sacred pause between effort and outcome.

This is a time to acknowledge your labor honestly. Lammas asks you to recognize what has grown because of your choices, your persistence, and your willingness to tend what mattered. Some harvests may look abundant and clear. Others may feel smaller than expected. Both are worthy of reflection. Every result carries wisdom. Gratitude strengthens manifestation not by ignoring shortcomings, but by honoring what has taken root.

The waning moon supports discernment and gentle release. As light slowly decreases, you are invited to evaluate where your energy has been wisely invested and where it has scattered. What projects have flourished? Which have drained more than they yielded? This awareness allows you to adjust without harshness, conserving resources for the turning season ahead. Manifestation at Lammas is not about demanding more. It is about honoring enough.

Earth governs this sabbat, grounding you in the physical reality of nourishment and support. Touch soil. Bake bread. Prepare food with herbs grown or chosen intentionally. Lammas reminds you that abundance is not theoretical. It is tangible, tasted, shared. The Earth's gifts require participation. You plant, you water, you weed, you wait. Then you gather. This cycle fosters humility and appreciation.

Historically, Lammas was a time of communal feasting and offering. The first loaves of bread were blessed and shared, symbolizing both gratitude and responsibility. Abundance must circulate to remain alive. In modern practice, sharing may look like offering food, supporting a friend, donating time, or teaching what you have learned. Generosity keeps prosperity moving rather than stagnant.

The herbs of Lammas support comfort, stability, and intentional manifestation. Basil encourages prosperity and purposeful action, reminding you to continue tending what thrives. Chamomile soothes and restores emotional balance after seasons of effort. Oatstraw nourishes deeply over time, strengthening resilience. Cinnamon brings warmth and activation, sparking confidence for the months ahead. Bay seals intentions and honors achievement. Together, these herbs are ideal for food magic, blessing rituals, and grounded manifestation work.

Lammas also carries the wisdom of sacrifice. To harvest is to cut. To gather grain is to end one stage of growth so another may begin. This sabbat gently asks what must be released to sustain future abundance. Are there habits, commitments, or expectations that no longer serve your highest path? Letting go now creates space for the deeper harvests still to come in autumn.

This is not a loud festival of beginning, but a steady acknowledgment of fruition. It teaches satisfaction without complacency and gratitude without attachment. You are invited to stand in the field of your own efforts and say, with humility and pride, this is what I have grown.

Ritual Idea:

Bake bread or craft an herbal salt using basil, cinnamon, and crushed bay leaf. As you mix or knead, focus on gratitude for what has manifested in your life.

Bless it by saying:

"I give thanks for what has come to fruition."
Share it with others if possible, sealing the energy of abundance through generosity and appreciation.

Mabon (Autumn Equinox, September 21–23)
The Scales of the Harvest

Theme: Reflection, gratitude, balance, and preparation for rest.
Moon: Waning
Element: Earth + Water
Herbs: Sage, Marigold, Apple, Mugwort, Rosemary

Mabon marks the second harvest and the return of balance, as day and night stand equal once more. The brightness of summer fades into softer light, and the Earth begins to turn inward. This sabbat is a sacred pause, inviting reflection on what has been gathered and what must now be released.

At Mabon, gratitude deepens through awareness. You are encouraged to look honestly at the season behind you, honoring both growth and loss. What has served its purpose may be thanked and laid to rest. What remains worthy of tending can be carried forward with intention. Balance is not about perfection here, but about conscious choice.

Earth and Water blend at Mabon, grounding reflection in emotion and memory. Earth reminds us of what sustains us physically, while Water carries feelings, intuition, and the wisdom of release. Together, they support gentle letting go, emotional clarity, and preparation for the quieter months ahead.

The waning moon reinforces this inward turning. This is a time to simplify, conserve energy, and close open loops. Cleansing rituals become acts of completion rather than renewal, clearing space so rest can be fully embraced. Mabon teaches that rest is not withdrawal, but preparation.

The herbs of Mabon hold both grounding and visionary qualities. Sage clears stagnant energy and honors wisdom earned. Marigold offers protection and remembrance. Apple symbolizes balance, abundance, and the cycles of life. Mugwort enhances intuition and dreamwork, while rosemary supports clarity and memory. These herbs are well-suited for reflective rituals, divination, and gentle cleansing.

Mabon invites you to prepare for descent. Just as the land sheds excess growth, you are asked to release expectations, habits, or attachments that no longer align. This shedding is not loss, but alignment with the natural rhythm of contraction.

Mabon also invites reconciliation within yourself. Where have you been out of balance, leaning too far into doing or too far into avoidance? The equal light and dark of the equinox mirror your own need for integration. This is a powerful time to forgive yourself for unfinished plans, unmet expectations, or perceived shortcomings. The harvest is rarely perfect, yet it is always enough. In accepting what is, you restore inner equilibrium.

There is quiet beauty in this season's descent. The air cools. Leaves begin their slow surrender. Nature models graceful release without resistance. Mabon teaches that letting go is not an act of defeat, but an act of wisdom. When you consciously release what has completed its cycle, you create spaciousness for winter's deep rest and future rebirth. In this sacred balance, you remember that contraction is not an ending. It is the necessary inhale before renewal begins again.

Ritual Idea:
Brew apple cider with cinnamon and sage. Sip slowly, reflecting on the year's lessons.
"As leaves fall, I release with grace."

Samhain (October 31–November 1)
The Thinning Veil

Theme: Ancestors, death, release, and inner truth.
Moon: Dark
Element: Water
Herbs: Mugwort, Wormwood, Rosemary, Yarrow, Cedar

Samhain marks the threshold between the light half and the dark half of the year. It is the witch's New Year, a liminal moment when endings and beginnings exist side by side. The veil between worlds grows thin, not as something to fear, but as an invitation to listen more closely to what is unseen.

This sabbat honors death as transformation rather than loss. It is a time to release what has completed its cycle, whether habits, identities, or griefs carried too long. Samhain asks for honesty and courage, inviting you to face your inner truth and claim the wisdom found in darkness.

Water governs Samhain, guiding emotion, memory, and intuition. Feelings may surface more strongly now, and dreams may grow vivid or symbolic. Divination practices are especially potent during this time, offering insight into both the future and the deeper layers of the self.

The dark moon supports inward reflection and deep release. This is a moment to pause, to rest, and to honor the stillness before rebirth. Samhain teaches that silence is fertile, and that clarity often arises when outer noise fades away.

The dark moon supports inward reflection and deep release. This is a moment to pause, to rest, and to honor the stillness before rebirth. Samhain teaches that silence is fertile, and that clarity often arises when outer noise fades away.

The herbs of Samhain carry protective and visionary energy. Mugwort enhances intuition and dreamwork. Wormwood supports boundary setting and release. Rosemary honors remembrance and continuity. Yarrow offers protection and courage, while cedar cleanses, grounds, and creates sacred space. Together, these herbs support ancestral connection, divination, and spiritual transition.

Samhain is also a time to honor those who came before you. Ancestors of blood, land, and spirit are remembered and thanked for the paths they opened. By acknowledging their presence, you strengthen your own sense of belonging and continuity.

Samhain also invites communion with the unseen aspects of yourself. The thinning veil is not only between worlds, but within your own psyche. Parts of you that were hidden, silenced, or set aside may rise now for acknowledgment. This is a powerful time for shadow work, journaling, and quiet contemplation. In the darkness, masks fall away. What remains is essence. Samhain asks you to sit with that essence without judgment, trusting that truth revealed in shadow becomes strength in the light.

There is profound peace in surrendering to this turning. As the land grows bare and the nights stretch long, you are reminded that emptiness is not absence, but preparation. The soil rests before it dreams of spring. Seeds lie dormant, gathering unseen energy. In honoring stillness and endings, you participate in the sacred cycle of renewal. Samhain teaches that every ending is also a doorway, and that in releasing with reverence, you create space for the next becoming to quietly take root.

Ritual Idea:

Light a candle for your ancestors. Offer herbs of remembrance like rosemary and yarrow.

Whisper: *"I remember, I release, I begin again."*

Yule (Winter Solstice, December 21–22)
The Return of Light

Theme: Rebirth, hope, rest, and renewal.
Moon: New
Element: Earth + Fire
Herbs: Cedar, Pine, Cinnamon, Clove, Orange Peel

Yule marks the longest night of the year, when darkness reaches its deepest point and the wheel turns once more toward the light. This sabbat honors the quiet miracle of return, not as sudden brightness, but as a subtle promise. From this night forward, the days will slowly lengthen, reminding us that even in stillness, change is already underway.

Yule is a sacred pause, inviting rest and reflection after the long descent of the dark season. It is not a time for effort or outward striving, but for restoration. The Earth lies dormant, conserving energy beneath frozen ground, and we are called to do the same. This is the season of deep listening, gentle warmth, and tending the inner hearth.

Earth and Fire combine at Yule, grounding us in stability while kindling hope. Earth holds us steady, offering safety and endurance, while Fire rekindles vitality and intention. Together, they teach us how to rest without stagnation and dream without urgency.

The new moon aligns perfectly with Yule's themes of rebirth and beginning. What is born now exists first as intention, vision, and quiet resolve. There is no pressure to act yet. Seeds planted in darkness are protected by it, gathering strength before emergence.

The herbs of Yule carry warmth, protection, and renewal. Cedar and pine cleanse and ground, connecting us to evergreen endurance. Cinnamon and clove spark warmth, comfort, and vitality, while orange peel brings lightness, joy, and the promise of returning Sun. These herbs are well-suited for warming teas, incense, and hearth rituals.

Yule invites gratitude for both light and dark. The darkness is not something to escape, but something that has shaped and strengthened you. By honoring what the dark season has offered, you make space to welcome what is coming with clarity and trust.

Yule is also a time to tend the flame within. While outer light is minimal, inner light becomes sacred. What belief has carried you through the dark months? What quiet strength has sustained you? This sabbat asks you to honor your resilience. The returning Sun mirrors your own capacity to endure, to soften without breaking, and to trust that warmth will come again. Even the smallest spark, carefully protected, is enough to illuminate the longest night.

There is profound magic in simplicity during this season. A warm drink held in steady hands. The scent of evergreen in the air. The glow of candlelight against winter's stillness. Yule teaches that renewal does not begin with grand declarations, but with quiet devotion. In resting deeply and dreaming gently, you prepare the soil of your spirit for what will eventually bloom. The light returns slowly, and so do you, strengthened by stillness and guided by hope.

Ritual Idea:
Create a Yule log or candle decorated with pine, cinnamon, and dried orange.
Light it as you speak gratitude for the darkness and hope for the coming light.
"From stillness I rise; from darkness, I grow."

The Living Cycle

The Wheel never stops turning, even when its movement feels invisible. Beneath the surface of stillness, change is always in motion. Roots grow in darkness. Ice melts slowly from within. Seeds swell before they ever break the soil. Seasons shift, light waxes and wanes, and life continues its quiet transformation. To recognize this truth is to release the illusion of stagnation and trust the rhythm that carries all things forward.

Each season prepares you for the next, offering lessons that unfold in their own time. Growth teaches you how to tend with consistency and hope. Harvest teaches you how to receive with gratitude and humility. Release teaches you how to let go with grace. Rest teaches you how to listen deeply and restore your strength. No phase exists in isolation. Each ending carries the seed of a beginning, waiting patiently for the right conditions to emerge.

To walk this cycle consciously is to live in relationship rather than resistance. It is the practice of meeting each season as it arrives, without clinging to what has passed or rushing toward what is yet to come. It is learning to recognize when you are in a personal winter and allowing yourself to rest without shame, or noticing when your inner spring calls for courage and fresh action. In this way, harmony is not something you strive for, but something you remember.

You are not separate from the Wheel. You are both seed and soil, flame and ash, bloom and root. You carry within you the same cycles of expansion and contraction, creation and dissolution, light and shadow. There will be seasons when you feel radiant and visible, and others when you feel quiet and unseen. Both are sacred. When you honor these rhythms within yourself, you move through life with greater ease and authenticity.

Herbal practice becomes a mirror of this living cycle. When you harvest in season, prepare with intention, and rest when the land rests, your work aligns naturally with the energy available to you. Plants gathered at their peak carry different qualities than those gathered in dormancy. Teas brewed for winter warmth differ from infusions meant for spring cleansing. The plants respond because they recognize your awareness. Magic flows not from effort, but from attunement.

Working with the Wheel teaches patience and trust. Not every desire is meant to manifest immediately, and not every pause is a delay. Some intentions require darkness to root deeply. Some healing requires quiet restoration before strength returns. When you honor timing rather than forcing outcomes, you allow wisdom to shape your path. What unfolds naturally tends to endure.

The Living Cycle also dissolves comparison. Just as no two gardens bloom at the same pace, no two lives unfold identically. Your season may not mirror another's. Your winter may last longer. Your harvest may arrive unexpectedly. Trusting the Wheel means trusting your own timing. When you stop measuring your growth against others, you reclaim the sacredness of your unique rhythm.

As your practice deepens, alignment no longer feels like something to pursue. It becomes something you inhabit. The need to force, fix, or chase begins to soften, replaced by a steady sense of belonging within the greater pattern of life. You feel the turning not as pressure, but as guidance.

You do not need to chase alignment. You are alignment. The Wheel turns, and you turn with it, rooted and radiant, shedding and becoming, resting and rising. In remembering this, you step fully into the living cycle, not as an observer, but as an active participant in the sacred rhythm of all things.

Reflection & Journaling Prompts

Which sabbat or season do you feel most connected to?

What do you notice about your energy through each phase
of the year?

How can you bring seasonal awareness into your daily
routines?

Reflection & Journaling Prompts

What herbs, scents, or rituals remind you of each turning of the Wheel?

How might you celebrate change as sacred rather than resisting it?

Ritual: The Green Wheel Blessing

You'll need:
- A candle for each element (green = earth, yellow = air, red = fire, blue = water, and white = Spirit)
- A small bowl of soil, water, a feather, and a spark of flame (or candle)
- A fresh herb from your garden or cupboard

Steps:

Arrange your candles in a circle to represent the Wheel of the Year. Light each one in turn, calling upon its

Element:
- *"Earth, ground me in your wisdom."*
- *"Air, clear my mind with truth."*
- *"Fire, ignite my courage."*
- *"Water, open my heart."*

Hold your herb and whisper:
"As the Wheel turns, so do I in rhythm, in grace, in gratitude."

Spend a moment in stillness.

Visualize yourself walking through each season, balanced and radiant.

When you're done, extinguish the candles in reverse order, giving thanks to each Element.

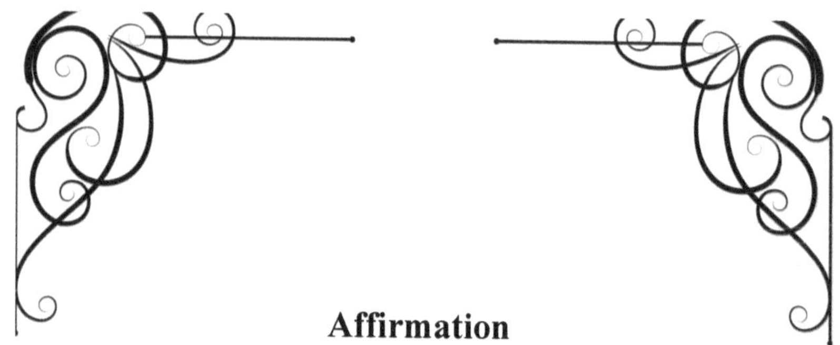

Affirmation
"I flow with the seasons and shine with the
Moon.
My roots deepen, my spirit blooms.
The Wheel turns, and I turn with it,
ever changing, ever whole."

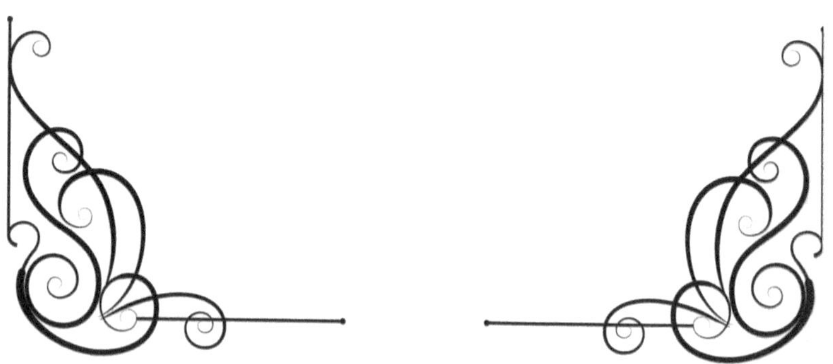

Advanced Herbal Alchemy:
The Art of Elemental and Energetic Blending
Invocation: The Alchemist's Fire

Alchemy is the sacred art of transformation, of turning raw material into revelation and the ordinary into the divine. Every potion, salve, or tea is more than matter; it is intention given form, prayer made tangible. Through heat, patience, and devotion, the witch participates in the ancient dance of change, guiding substance from one state into another. In this act, she remembers that transformation is the natural language of the universe.

To practice herbal alchemy is to honor the unity between the seen and unseen, between Earth and Ether. Roots and resins, leaves and petals carry physical properties, yet they also hold memory, vibration, and spirit. The alchemist works at this meeting point, where chemistry and consciousness intertwine. Precision becomes reverence. Intuition becomes guidance. Science and spirit are not opposites here, but partners in sacred creation.

The Alchemist's Fire burns both within and without. It is the flame beneath the vessel and the spark within the heart. It is focus, clarity, and willingness to be changed by the work itself. As herbs soften, infuse, and release their essence, so too does the witch refine her own awareness. The fire does not only transform the blend. It transforms the one who tends it.

Here, the witch becomes both cauldron and catalyst, both vessel and flame. She understands that every act of blending mirrors an inner process of integration. As above, so below. As within, so the garden grows. In calling upon the Alchemist's Fire, she opens herself to conscious transformation, trusting that what is tended with patience and love will emerge luminous, balanced, and alive.

The Alchemist's Circle

You have walked the spiral of seasons, tended the garden of your spirit, and listened to the song of leaf and root. The Earth has taught you her rhythms, the Moon has shown you her tides, and the Elements have whispered their secrets in wind and flame.

Now you stand at the threshold of mastery. The circle turns again, not outward but inward, calling you to blend everything you have learned into living wisdom.

Here begins the work of the alchemist. It is not simply about creating potions or tinctures, but about weaving energy, emotion, and intention into form. It is about transformation, both within and without. The herbs that once taught you to heal and protect now teach you to transmute and elevate.

Every blend becomes a mirror of your inner state, every flame a reminder that creation and change are the same sacred fire. To practice alchemy is to remember that you, too, are made of the same elements that stir the stars and awaken the soil.

Step into the circle. Light your candle. Open your heart to the mystery of creation, and let your craft become the prayer that unites Earth and Spirit.

The circle is open, yet unbroken.
Blessed be the hands that create.

The Spirit of Herbal Alchemy

Every herb carries an energetic signature, a living vibration shaped by color, scent, texture, and purpose. These signatures are formed through the plant's relationship with sun and soil, rain and wind, and the long memory of the land where it grows. A plant that thrives in harsh, rocky terrain carries resilience. One that unfurls delicate blossoms at dawn holds a different kind of medicine. When you work with herbs, you are not simply combining ingredients; you are entering into conversation with distinct energies that wish to be acknowledged and understood.

To sense these signatures requires more than intellectual knowledge. It asks you to observe how a plant makes you feel. Does it warm or cool? Expand or contract? Soothe or stimulate? The body often understands before the mind does. The scent of rosemary may sharpen awareness instantly. Chamomile may soften the breath without effort. These responses are clues, guiding you toward deeper understanding of the plant's subtle character.

Conscious blending is the art of listening for harmony. When herbs are brought together with intention, their individual songs merge into a unified frequency, one that resonates with your desired outcome. Some blends sing softly, offering comfort and restoration. Others hum with protective strength or pulse with transformative fire. The witch learns to sense balance instinctively, adjusting ratios not only for flavor or potency, but for energetic cohesion. A blend is complete when it feels steady, when its presence carries clarity rather than discord.

Elemental awareness deepens this practice. Earth herbs ground and stabilize. Water herbs soothe and open emotion. Air herbs clarify thought and perception. Fire herbs activate and inspire.

When these forces are layered with care, a preparation becomes multidimensional. You are not only addressing a symptom or intention; you are creating a balanced current that flows through body, mind, and spirit simultaneously.

True alchemy does not occur solely in the glass jar or the simmering pot. It unfolds within the witch herself. As you prepare teas, oils, tinctures, and charms, your attention shapes the work. Your breath slows. Your posture softens. Your awareness sharpens. You begin to notice subtle shifts in energy as herbs release their essence. This inner transformation is not secondary to the practice. It is the heart of it.

When you infuse herbs with purpose, you are also infusing yourself with intention. Each act of preparation becomes a ritual of alignment, where thought, feeling, and action move as one. The change that occurs within you subtly alters the outcome, anchoring the magic in lived experience rather than abstract desire. This is why presence matters more than perfection. A simple tea prepared with reverence carries more potency than an elaborate blend made in distraction.

Over time, the relationship between you and the plants deepens. You begin to sense when an herb calls to be included. You recognize which allies support one another and which combinations require moderation. The process becomes intuitive without abandoning knowledge. Study informs instinct. Instinct refines study. This reciprocity is the hallmark of advanced herbal alchemy.

The Green Witch's tools remain humble: a bowl, a candle, time, and devotion. Yet within these simple forms lives profound power. Her true magic lies in awareness, the ability to feel how one herb calls to another, how scent becomes story, and how intention becomes elixir. In this way, herbal alchemy is not something she performs. It is something she embodies, again and again, through attentive, loving practice.

Blending Herbs & Understanding Combinations

Blending herbs is both science and poetry.
It's the art of creating harmony between energies,
elements, and planetary influences.

When crafting blends, consider the **trinity of balance:**
The Base Herb:
your foundation. Grounding, stabilizing, usually Earth or
Water element. (Example: chamomile, rose, or oatstraw.)

The Catalyst Herb: the activator that adds movement or
focus. Often Fire or Air element. (Example: cinnamon for
vitality, peppermint for clarity.)

The Bridge Herb: the harmonizer that links the blend
together and smooths transitions. (Example: lavender or
lemon balm.)

A well-balanced blend addresses **body, mind, and spirit.**
For example: a grounding tea may include chamomile
(calm), peppermint (clarity), and cinnamon (warmth and
flow).
You'll feel when the energy clicks, the scent will "sing,"
the energy will hum in your hands.

Trust your intuition; the plants are speaking through it.

Methods of Preparation

Each preparation method draws out a different layer of a plant's medicine, physical, emotional, or energetic.

Infusions (Teas):
- Use leaves and flowers.
- Pour hot water over herbs, cover, and steep for 5–10 minutes.
- Best for emotional healing, heart-opening, and daily rituals.

Decoctions:
- For roots, barks, and dense herbs.
- Simmer gently for 20–30 minutes.
- Ideal for grounding, stamina, or protection spells.

Tinctures:
- Soak herbs in alcohol for 4–6 weeks.
- Extracts deep plant compounds and spirit essence.
- Best for long-term vitality and focus.

Elixirs:
- Blend tincture with honey or syrup.
- A heart-centered medicine of sweetness and strength.
- Perfect for emotional healing, courage, and creativity.

Oils:
- Infuse herbs in carrier oil (olive, jojoba, or almond) for 2–4 weeks in sunlight or moonlight.
- Strain and use for anointing, massage, or candle dressing.
- If you use essential oils, I suggest **do NOT ingest**

Salves & Balms:
- Combine infused oils with beeswax or cocoa butter.
- Creates protective, soothing, or healing ointments for the body and energy field.

Powders & Incense:
- Ground dried herbs with intention.
- Use in spell sachets, charms, or to dress candles and offerings.

Each method corresponds to an Element:
Earth: Salves, balms, grounding blends.
Air: Incense, smokes, and breath-based rituals.
Fire: Tinctures, decoctions, and transformation work.
Water: Teas, elixirs, emotional healing.

The Planetary Keys

Each planet lends its essence to herbs and magic. When you align with their energy, your potions and rituals become attuned to universal flow.

Planet	Energy & Focus	Herbs	Day	Element
Sun	Vitality, confidence, illumination	St. John's Wort, Calendula, Rosemary	Sunday	Fire
Moon	Intuition, dreams, emotional healing	Mugwort, Jasmine, Chamomile	Monday	Water
☿ Mercury	Communication, intellect, movement	Lavender, Peppermint, Lemongrass	Wednesday	Air
♀ Venus	Love, beauty, harmony	Rose, Hibiscus, Apple Blossom	Friday	Water
♂ Mars	Action, courage, protection	Basil, Cinnamon, Ginger	Tuesday	Fire
♃ Jupiter	Abundance, growth, wisdom	Sage, Oak, Bay Leaf	Thursday	Earth
♄ Saturn	Discipline, grounding, boundaries	Patchouli, Vetiver, Cypress	Saturday	Earth

Each planetary correspondence acts as a tuning fork for your work. To create an elixir for courage, for example, you might combine Mars herbs (basil, cinnamon) during the Waxing Moon on a Tuesday, layering Fire and growth.

Charging & Empowering Your Blends

Herbs hold innate energy, but your intention animates it. Charging your blends bridges human will and natural spirit.

Moonlight:
Place your blends or oils beneath the appropriate moon phase, waxing for attraction, waning for release, full for empowerment.

Sunlight:
Charge vitality blends or solar elixirs under the morning sun for courage, warmth, and radiance.

Sound:
Chant, sing, or use bells, singing bowls, or gentle drumming to activate frequency and clear stagnant energy.

Sigils & Symbols:
Draw protective or empowering sigils on jars, bottles, or labels to imprint purpose into the vibration of your blend.

Visualization:
Hold your herbs between your palms. Picture golden-white light flowing from your heart through your hands, infusing your blend with life force and love.

Each act of intention amplifies the herbal magic, turning it into a co-created spell.

Ethical Harvesting & Sourcing

The Earth gives abundantly, but magic rooted in respect grows stronger.

Harvest mindfully: Take only what you need, never more than one-third of a plant or patch. Always leave offerings, water, a whispered blessing, a strand of hair, or a song.

Source sustainably: Buy from small, ethical herb farms, local apothecaries, or grow your own when possible. Avoid overharvested or endangered species.

Honor the spirit: Speak to your plants before harvesting. Ask permission and thank them afterward. Their energy stays purer when treated as kin, not a commodity.

Reciprocity: For every herb you harvest, plant or give something back. The balance of taking and giving is the essence of Green Witch ethics.

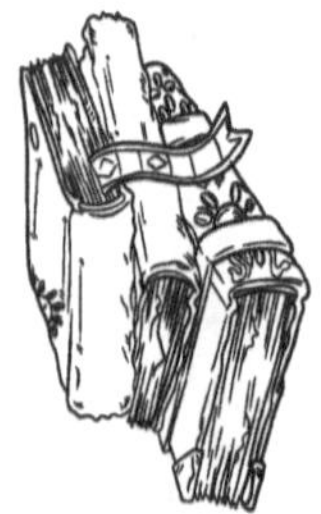

Creating Herbal Elixirs & Oils

Elixirs and oils are the heart of advanced alchemy, where intention, element, and emotion merge into living energy.

To Create an Elixir:

Combine herbs in a glass jar. Cover halfway with brandy or apple cider vinegar.

Add honey or maple syrup for sweetness and preservation.

Infuse for one lunar cycle, shaking daily while visualizing the blend absorbing your intention.

Strain and bottle. Label with name, date, and purpose.

Use a few drops under the tongue, in tea, or anoint your wrists during ritual.

To Create an Infused Oil:

Add herbs to a clean jar, filling halfway.

Cover completely with oil.

Infuse in sunlight (for vitality) or moonlight (for intuition) for 2–4 weeks.

Strain and use as anointing oil, bath oil, or ritual blend.

These are not just tools, they are **vessels of transformation.**

Each one carries your energy, your story, and your devotion.

Reflection & Journaling Prompts

Which planetary and elemental energies most influence your magic?

____

____

____

____

How do you feel when blending herbs? Do certain ones call to you more strongly?

____

____

____

____

____

What ethical practices can you incorporate to deepen your connection with the Earth?

____

____

____

____

____

____

Reflection & Journaling Prompts

How might charging your blends change the way you approach ritual?

____

____

____

____

____

____

____

____

What elixir, oil, or potion would best represent your energy right now, and why?

____

____

____

____

____

____

____

____

Ritual: The Alchemist's Light

Purpose: To create a charged herbal elixir that embodies your intention and connects you to planetary harmony.

You'll need:
A small glass jar
A mix of herbs chosen by element and planet
Honey and brandy (or vinegar)
A candle matching your goal (gold for vitality, silver for intuition, green for growth)
A bowl of salt and a feather or incense for cleansing

Steps:
Cleanse your space with salt and smoke.
Light your candle and speak your intention aloud.
Add herbs to your jar, one by one, saying:
> *"By root and bloom, by fire and sea,*
> *I blend the world within and me."*

Pour brandy and honey over the herbs. Stir clockwise with a clean spoon.
Hold the jar in your hands. Visualize it glowing with golden light. Whisper gratitude to each plant and planet.
Seal and label. Charge under the appropriate moon phase for one lunar cycle.

Use this elixir sparingly in ritual or meditation to anchor your intention into daily life.

Affirmation
"I am the vessel of transformation.
My craft is a harmony of Earth and star.
Through my hands, the old becomes new,
and in every blend, I find myself reborn."

Earthbound Allies:
Working with Stones and Crystals.
"Some magic moves like breath. Some magic stays."

Invocation: Earthbound Allies

I call to the bones of the Earth,
to the stones that remember fire and pressure,
to the quiet ones who have held their shape through ages
unseen. I stand upon you now with reverence,
acknowledging the deep time that lives within your form,
the wisdom shaped long before my voice was born.
Ancient ones of crystal and stone, you who were forged in
darkness and light, in heat and stillness, in breaking and
becoming, I ask your presence as I enter this work.
Not as tools to command, but as allies to walk beside me,
steady and enduring, holding what must be held and grounding
what seeks form.
Teach me the language of weight and patience.
Teach me how to anchor intention without force, how to build
magic that lasts, how to listen for truth that does not shout.
Where herbs move like breath and blood, show me how to
work with stillness, how to trust the slow shaping of purpose.
May this chapter be guided by respect, by ethical hands and
mindful choice, by remembrance that every stone carries a
story and every crystal has traveled far to arrive here. Let my
magic be rooted, my boundaries clear, my rituals anchored in
balance between Earth and spirit.
With gratitude, I open this space. With intention, I step onto the
stone path. May the Earthbound Allies witness this work,
strengthen what is true, and hold steady what is meant to
endure.
So it is.

The Bones of the Earth

If herbs are the breath of the Earth, stones are her bones.

They are older than memory, shaped by pressure, fire, water, and spans of time beyond human reckoning. Mountains rise and erode. Rivers carve valleys. Volcanoes cool into obsidian and basalt. Crystals form slowly in darkness, their geometry unfolding in silence. Stones do not hurry. They do not bloom and fade like plants. They endure, holding the deep rhythm of the planet within their structure. When you hold a stone, you hold condensed time.

Stones carry the memory of formation. Granite remembers compression and heat. Quartz remembers clarity born of pressure. River stones remember movement and smoothing through persistence. Each carries a story written in mineral and pattern. When you work with them, you are not asking for something foreign. You are aligning with qualities already embodied in their structure: stability, resilience, clarity, grounding, amplification.

In Root and Ritual work, stones and crystals serve as stabilizers, anchors, and witnesses. They ground magic into form. A crystal placed on an altar holds intention steadily, even when your focus shifts. A stone carried in a pocket reminds you of strength long after the ritual flame has dimmed. They remember what we ask of them, not through sentiment, but through energetic imprint. They hold space long after a ritual has ended, quietly continuing the work we began.

Where herbs move quickly through infusion and smoke, stones move slowly and consistently. Their medicine is subtle but enduring. They support long-term intentions, boundary setting, emotional steadiness, and protection.

If herbs are like breath moving through the body, stones are like the skeleton beneath the skin, providing structure and containment. They remind us that not all magic must be dynamic. Some magic is simply presence.

Working with stones invites a different kind of relationship than working with plants. There is less harvesting and more stewardship. Stones are gathered thoughtfully, chosen intuitively, and cared for respectfully. Cleansing may involve water, smoke, sunlight, or moonlight, but always with awareness of the stone's nature. This is not about collecting endlessly. It is about forming meaningful connections with a few steady allies.

Stones also teach boundaries. Their solidity mirrors the importance of energetic containment. A protective stone placed at a doorway reinforces intention. A grounding stone held during meditation anchors wandering thoughts. A boundary is not a wall of fear, but a foundation of self-respect. Stones embody this lesson effortlessly. They remain themselves, unchanged by external pressure, steady in their form.

While herbs teach us about cycles, change, and responsiveness, stones teach us about patience, endurance, and permanence. Together, they form a balanced partnership that honors both motion and stillness, growth and containment. In ritual, pairing plant and stone unites breath and bone, flow and form. One carries intention outward. The other roots it deeply.

To work with the bones of the Earth is to remember your own. You, too, have structure beneath softness. You, too, carry ancient resilience in your body and spirit. When you sit with stone in hand, you align with steadiness that predates language and outlasts doubt. This chapter explores how to work with stones and crystals in a grounded, respectful, and intentional way, not as decorative trends, but as ancient allies in your practice, steady companions in the sacred rhythm of Root and Ritual.

The Spirit and Energy of Stones

Every stone carries an energetic signature shaped by its origin and formation. Some are born in fire, forged deep within the Earth under immense heat and pressure, emerging through volcanic force or tectonic shift. Others are shaped slowly by water, sediment, and time, formed grain by grain through patience rather than upheaval. These origins matter, not only geologically, but energetically, imprinting each stone with a rhythm, a temperament, and a way of moving magic through the world.

Fire-born stones carry the pulse of transformation. Their energy is activating, protective, and often uncompromising. They resonate with courage, boundary-setting, and the dissolution of what no longer serves. In ritual, these stones support moments of change, initiation, and deep personal alchemy. They remind the witch that creation is often born from pressure and that sacred fire both destroys and reshapes.

Water-shaped stones move with a quieter power. Formed through erosion, flow, and persistence, they hold the wisdom of yielding without surrender. Their energy soothes and harmonizes, opening pathways for emotional healing, intuition, dreamwork, and remembrance. These stones teach the magic of soft strength, of listening deeply, and of trusting the currents that guide us beneath conscious thought.

Dense, iron-rich stones anchor the spirit to the body and the body to the Earth. Their weight carries protective magic, drawing excess energy downward and reinforcing energetic boundaries. In ritual work, they serve as guardians and stabilizers, particularly during shadow work, ancestral exploration, or moments of emotional upheaval. These stones hold steady when the world feels unbalanced, offering containment rather than escape.

Clear crystalline stones act as conduits of intention. Their internal structure allows energy to move with clarity and coherence, amplifying what is placed within them. They do not impose direction, but they do reflect with precision. In magic, they ask for honesty and focus, mirroring the truth of your intention back into the world.

Unlike herbs, which often act swiftly and visibly, stones do not push energy outward. They do not hurry or bloom. They hold. They absorb, stabilize, and reflect, continuing their work long after the ritual space has been closed. This makes them powerful allies in long-term spellwork, protection, altar magic, and any ritual meant to anchor intention into form.

Stones are keepers of memory. Each use leaves an imprint, layering intention upon intention like sediment building over time. A stone worked with consistently becomes attuned not only to its natural essence, but to the witch who works with it. Such stones carry the resonance of shared practice, holding what has been asked of them with quiet devotion.

When you work with stones, you are not commanding energy or shaping power through force. You are entering into relationship with something ancient, something that understands endurance. Stones know how to remain. They know how to hold their place through fire, water, and time.

In their presence, the witch learns that magic does not always move. Sometimes it roots. Sometimes it waits. Sometimes it simply is, steady and unyielding, until the moment arrives for change to take form.

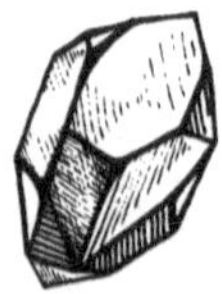

Why Stones Are Used in Ritual Work

Stones appear in magical traditions across cultures and centuries for good reason. Their roles are consistent, reliable, and deeply practical.

Anchoring and Grounding

Ritual work can raise energy quickly. Stones help bring that energy back into the body and into the Earth, preventing spiritual fatigue or imbalance.

Protection and Boundary Creation

Many stones form energetic shields, reinforcing boundaries around people, homes, and sacred spaces.

Amplification and Focus

Crystals can magnify intention, directing energy with clarity and precision when paired with herbs, candles, or spoken words.

Memory and Continuity

Unlike herbs, which must be replenished, stones retain energetic impressions. A stone used repeatedly for a specific purpose becomes a living record of your work.

Elemental Balance

Stones are deeply aligned with the Earth element, offering balance when rituals involve Fire, Air, or Water energies.

Building Relationship with Stone Allies

Stones are not objects to be collected and set aside. They are not simply correspondences in a list or ingredients in a spell. Like herbs, they respond best when treated as allies, and like any ally, relationship must be cultivated.

To work with a stone is to enter into quiet partnership.

Before placing a stone into ritual, spend time in its presence. Hold it in your hands without expectation. Sit with it in stillness. Notice its weight and how it rests in your palm. Feel its temperature, its smoothness or roughness, its edges or curves. Observe the way light moves across its surface. Let your senses attune before your mind begins assigning meaning.

Pay attention to your body. Does your breathing shift? Does your spine straighten? Does your chest soften? Some stones ground you immediately, pulling scattered energy downward. Others lift your awareness subtly upward, opening intuitive channels. Some may feel steady and neutral at first, like a stone standing quietly at the edge of the circle, watching. That neutrality is not absence. It is patience.

Some stones reveal themselves gradually. Their presence unfolds layer by layer, deepening as trust builds. Others announce themselves from the first touch, resonating strongly and unmistakably. Neither experience is more powerful than the other. The pace of revelation is part of the relationship itself.

Consider sleeping with a stone near your bed for a few nights before using it in ritual. Carry it with you for a day and observe how your mood, thoughts, or interactions subtly shift. Place it beside you during meditation without giving it a task. Allow it to exist with you before asking it to work for you.

Naming a stone can strengthen connection, especially if it becomes a long-term ritual companion. The name does not need to be elaborate. It may arise naturally after time together. Dedication also deepens relationship. You might hold the stone and speak its purpose aloud, inviting it into partnership for protection, clarity, healing, or transformation.

Placing a stone regularly on your altar establishes continuity. The altar becomes a shared space, and the stone begins to hold the energetic rhythm of your practice. Over time, it absorbs not only intention, but atmosphere. It learns the tone of your prayers, the cadence of your rituals, the frequency of your magic.

As relationship deepens, the stone becomes attuned not only to its inherent qualities but to you. It begins to respond differently in your hands than it would in another's. It carries your energetic imprint, just as you carry a subtle awareness of its presence.

Respect is essential in this partnership. Cleanse and rest your stones when they feel heavy. Thank them after significant ritual work. Do not demand more than feels aligned. Stone allies are steady, but they are not inexhaustible. They deserve acknowledgment.

In building relationship with stone allies, you learn something profound about magic itself. Power does not need to be extracted. It can be shared. Support does not need to be forced. It can be invited.

And in the quiet companionship of Earth's oldest beings, you begin to understand that magic rooted in relationship is magic that endures.

Choosing Stones Intuitively and Practically

Choosing Stones Intuitively and Practically

There are countless stones and crystals available in the modern world. Shelves glitter with color and promise. Shops offer names, properties, origins, and elaborate correspondences. It can be tempting to believe that effective magic requires an extensive collection, each stone neatly categorized and ready for use.

It does not. You do not need many stones to work powerfully. You need relationship, clarity, and purpose.

Choosing stones is not about accumulation. It is about alignment.

Begin with intention. What season are you in? What kind of work are you doing? Protection? Healing? Confidence? Grief? Abundance? Focus? Let your current path guide your choices. A stone chosen for a specific purpose will serve you far more deeply than one chosen simply because it is beautiful or trending.

Then listen to your intuition. When you encounter a stone, notice what happens in your body before your mind begins analyzing. Does your breath soften? Do you feel steadier? Is there a quiet pull toward it? Intuition rarely shouts. It hums. The stone that belongs with you will often feel familiar rather than dramatic.

At the same time, practicality matters. Consider how often you will realistically use a stone. A crystal aligned with daily grounding or protection may serve you more consistently than one reserved for rare ceremonial workings. Choose stones that support your actual life, not just your ideal ritual self.

It is better to have a small collection you know well than a large collection that gathers dust. A handful of stones worked with repeatedly becomes energetically rich and deeply attuned. They begin to recognize your touch. They learn your rhythm. They carry the layered memory of your practice.

Excess, even in magic, can dilute focus.

Trust attraction, but also listen carefully to resistance. Sometimes resistance signals growth. Other times it signals misalignment. If a stone feels heavy, overwhelming, sharp, or unsettling in a way that lingers, honor that sensation. You may not be ready for its lessons, or it may not be meant for you at all.

Not every powerful stone is appropriate for every practitioner. Some stones are intense teachers. Others are gentle companions. Both are valuable, but discernment protects your energy and your practice.

You may also find that your relationship with certain stones changes over time. A crystal that once supported you may feel complete in its work. Another may suddenly call to you during a life transition. This is natural. As you evolve, so do your allies.

When choosing stones, consider ethical sourcing as part of the decision. Ask where the stone comes from. Consider how it was mined. Choose transparency when possible. Magic rooted in exploitation weakens the very intention it seeks to strengthen. A smaller, ethically sourced collection carries far more integrity than a large, carelessly acquired one.

Above all, remember that stones are Earth's ancient bodies. They do not require urgency. They do not compete. They are not scarce in spirit, even if rare in form.

Choose slowly. Choose thoughtfully. Choose with reverence. And trust that the stones meant to walk beside you will remain.

Ways to Work with Stones in Ritual

Stones are versatile and adaptable. Below are foundational methods that integrate seamlessly into Root and Ritual practices.

Altar Stones

Place stones on your altar to anchor intentions and guard sacred space. These stones hold the ongoing energy of your work even when you are not actively practicing.

Ritual Holding Stones

Holding a stone during prayer, spellwork, or meditation helps focus intention and ground excess energy.

Spell Jars and Containers

Adding stones or crystal chips to spell jars anchors the magic and extends its lifespan.

Circle and Boundary Stones

Place stones at the edges of ritual space, doorways, or land boundaries for protection and containment.

Ongoing Companions

Carry stones with you during periods of focused intention, such as healing work, transformation, or protection.

Cleansing and Caring for Stones

Stones absorb energy over time.

They hold intention, atmosphere, memory, and emotion. They anchor ritual work long after candles burn down and herbs return to ash. This capacity to hold is part of their power, but like all vessels, they benefit from clearing and renewal.

Cleansing is not about removing something "bad." It is about restoring balance. It is about releasing what no longer belongs so that the stone may return to its natural resonance.

Unlike herbs, stones do not fade quickly. They do not exhaust easily. Cleansing does not need to be constant or rigidly scheduled. Instead, learn to sense when it is needed. A stone may feel heavier than usual. Its surface may seem energetically muted. You may notice that it no longer responds the way it once did in your hand.

When a stone feels dull, heavy, clouded, or disconnected, it is usually time. Gentle methods are often best.

Moonlight is one of the simplest and most harmonious ways to cleanse stones. Placing them beneath the night sky allows lunar energy to wash through their structure. Full moons are potent, but any moon phase carries its own rhythm. New moon light renews. Full moon light amplifies and clears. Waning moonlight supports release.

Smoke from herbs or resins offers another time-honored method. Pass the stone slowly through the rising smoke of rosemary, cedar, frankincense, or ethically sourced sage. Allow the smoke to encircle and drift across the surface, imagining stagnant energy dissolving and lifting away. Smoke cleansing is especially effective after intense ritual work or emotional processing.

Sound clears without physical contact. Bells, chimes, singing bowls, drumming, or even steady chanting can break up stagnant energy patterns. Sound moves through crystalline structures easily, restoring clarity and flow. This method is especially useful for delicate stones that should not be exposed to moisture.

Earth contact reconnects the stone to its origin. Placing it directly on soil, beneath a tree, or nestled in a garden for a period of time allows excess energy to disperse naturally. The Earth does not struggle to rebalance what comes from her. She receives and restores with quiet steadiness.

Water is often suggested as a cleansing method, but not all stones tolerate moisture. Some dissolve, crack, or lose structural integrity. Salt, especially, can be abrasive or damaging. Avoid harsh methods unless you are certain the stone can withstand them. When in doubt, choose moonlight, smoke, sound, or earth. These are gentle, universally supportive approaches.

Cleansing is also an act of respect. It acknowledges that the stone has been working. It honors its participation in your practice. When you cleanse a stone, do so with presence rather than haste. Hold it briefly afterward. Notice if its energy feels lighter, clearer, or steadier.

After cleansing, re-dedication strengthens the bond between you. Hold the stone in both hands. Breathe slowly. Speak its purpose aloud or silently. You may say:

"I clear what no longer serves.

I renew this bond.

May you hold protection, clarity, grounding, or healing as we have agreed."

Rededication does not need to be elaborate. It is an affirmation of partnership.

There may also be times when a stone feels complete in its work with you. It may no longer respond or feel aligned. In such cases, consider resting it on your altar, returning it to the Earth, or gifting it to another practitioner who feels called to it. Relationships shift. Magic evolves.

Caring for stones is not maintenance in a mechanical sense. It is stewardship. It is tending to Earth's ancient bones with gratitude.

In cleansing and renewal, you honor not only the stone, but the continuity of your own practice. And in that rhythm of use, clearing, and re-dedication, the partnership deepens.

Stones and Crystals for Ritual Use

Below is a practical list of stones commonly used in Ritual work, along with their foundational purposes.

Clear Quartz

Amplification, clarity, intention-setting

Strengthens any spell or ritual it is included in.

Amethyst

Intuition, spiritual protection, emotional balance

Supports dream work, meditation, and psychic development.

Rose Quartz

Love, self-compassion, emotional healing

Encourages heart healing and gentle self-love magic.

Black Tourmaline

Protection, grounding, energy cleansing

Absorbs and neutralizes negative or intrusive energy.

Obsidian

Truth, shadow work, deep protection

Reveals hidden patterns and supports deep transformation.

Smoky Quartz

Grounding, stress relief, transmutation

Helps release anxiety and stabilize intense emotions.

Citrine

Abundance, confidence, manifestation

Attracts prosperity and strengthens personal power.

Carnelian

Creativity, courage, motivation

Supports action, confidence, and forward movement.

Moonstone

Intuition, emotional flow, lunar magic

Aligns with cycles, intuition, and feminine energy.

Hematite

Stability, grounding, mental clarity

Excellent for grounding after ritual or spiritual work.

Labradorite

Magic, transformation, psychic protection

Strengthens intuition while shielding the aura.

Selenite

Cleansing, clarity, spiritual connection

Clears stagnant energy and raises vibrational awareness.

Black Onyx

Protection, strength, emotional resilience

Provides steady support during difficult transitions.

Tiger's Eye

Confidence, courage, balanced power

Blends grounding with personal empowerment.

Green Aventurine

Growth, luck, emotional renewal

Supports new beginnings and gentle abundance work.

Lapis Lazuli

Wisdom, truth, inner vision

Enhances communication and spiritual insight.

Fluorite

Focus, mental clarity, energetic order

Organizes scattered thoughts and energy.

Pyrite

Protection, prosperity, vitality

Acts as a shield while attracting abundance.

Jade

Harmony, longevity, prosperity

Encourages balance, peace, and steady growth.

Malachite

Transformation, emotional release, protection

Assists with deep healing and energetic clearing.

Red Jasper

Strength, endurance, grounding

Stabilizes energy and supports physical vitality.

Blue Lace Agate

Calm communication, emotional soothing

Eases anxiety and supports gentle expression.

Howlite

Patience, awareness, emotional regulation

Calms an overactive mind and encourages mindfulness.

Lepidolite

Emotional balance, stress relief, transition

Excellent for soothing grief, anxiety, and change.

Garnet

Vitality, passion, grounding desire

Strengthens commitment, energy, and life force.

Stones in Seasonal and Cyclical Work

Magic does not live outside of time. It breathes through it.

Stones, with their ancient patience, are uniquely suited to cyclical practice. They understand duration. They understand repetition. They have witnessed more seasons than we will ever see. Glaciers have formed and melted around them. Forests have grown and fallen. Rivers have changed course. When you invite stones into seasonal or lunar work, you are aligning human intention with rhythms far older and steadier than your own. Their presence tempers urgency and deepens trust.

Unlike herbs, which bloom and wither within a single year, stones remain constant as the Wheel turns. This constancy makes them powerful companions for tracking growth over time. A stone placed on your altar at the New Moon and revisited at the Full Moon becomes a witness to your intentions. A crystal dedicated at the start of a season absorbs the subtle shifts of that entire phase. In this way, stones hold continuity, even as your life evolves.

Stones can be dedicated to seasons, moon phases, life passages, or long-term cycles of growth and transformation. In doing so, they become markers of time, holding the energetic imprint of a specific phase and anchoring it into form. A grounding stone used each winter may come to embody rest and introspection. A bright, activating crystal used each spring may hold the memory of renewal and courage. Over years, these stones become layered with meaning, carrying a living archive of your journey.

In lunar practice, stones are especially potent allies. A dark stone may accompany you during the New Moon, supporting inward reflection and seed planting. A luminous or clear stone may rest beside you at the Full Moon, amplifying insight and illumination. Returning to the same stones each cycle creates a rhythm of familiarity. The stone remembers the intention of past moons, and you begin to sense subtle patterns emerging across time.

Seasonal dedication deepens this bond further. You may choose one stone to represent each sabbat, placing it on your altar as the Wheel turns. Over the years, these stones accumulate the energy of repeated ritual, gratitude, release, and renewal. They become quiet companions to your spiritual calendar, embodying the steady movement of the year even when your own pace feels uncertain.

Stones are also powerful anchors during life transitions. When entering a new chapter, you may select a stone to carry through that passage. It becomes a tactile reminder of your commitment to growth. Each time you touch it, you reinforce the intention set at the beginning of the cycle. When the transition completes, the stone holds the memory of who you were and who you became.

Cyclical work with stones teaches patience. Transformation is rarely immediate. Like mineral formation deep within the Earth, change often occurs slowly, layer by layer. By working with stones over extended periods, you align with this slower tempo. You learn to trust that steady devotion shapes lasting results.

In honoring stones as seasonal allies, you root your practice in continuity. You acknowledge that magic unfolds within time, not apart from it. And as the Wheel turns again and again, your stones remain beside you, steady and enduring, witnesses to your becoming.

Lunar Work

The Moon offers one of the most accessible cycles for stone practice. Each phase carries a distinct energetic tone.

A stone placed on your altar for a full lunar cycle absorbs that rhythm gradually, night after night. It witnesses the waxing build of intention, the fullness of illumination, and the quiet release of the waning phase. When the cycle completes, that stone carries within it the memory of that journey.

You may dedicate:

- A stone for new moon intention-setting
- A different stone for full moon amplification
- A grounding stone for waning moon release

After one complete cycle, the stone becomes attuned to that specific phase and can be reused in future moon rituals, already resonant with that pattern. Over time, your lunar stones become deeply layered allies, holding not only cosmic rhythm but your personal evolution within it.

Some practitioners choose one stone per moon phase. Others work with a single lunar companion stone that remains on the altar month after month, absorbing the ebb and flow continuously. Both approaches are valid. The key is consistency and awareness.

Seasonal Work

Just as the Moon turns, so does the Wheel of the Year.

Stones may be rotated seasonally to ground the energy of each turning. A bright, solar stone may anchor summer altars. A grounding, inward-facing stone may serve during winter. Transitional stones may support spring emergence or autumn release.

As the Wheel turns, you physically shift the stones on your altar. This small act becomes ritual in itself. It signals change not only to the outer world, but to your inner landscape.

Seasonal stones act as energetic bookmarks. When you return to them year after year, they carry the echo of past seasons. The stone you placed on your altar during last winter's quiet introspection will feel different when it returns the following year. It will remember what was planted in the dark and what has since grown.

In this way, stones become witnesses to your cycles of death and rebirth, rest and action, contraction and expansion.

Life Cycles and Long-Term Intentions

Beyond lunar and seasonal rhythms, stones can also be dedicated to longer personal cycles. A stone may accompany you through a year of healing, a period of study, a creative project, or a significant life transition.

Placed on your altar or carried consistently, it absorbs the steady progression of that chapter. When the cycle closes, you may cleanse and re-dedicate the stone, or retire it as a marker of completion.

Some practitioners keep such stones as anchors of memory. Others return them to the Earth in gratitude. Both choices honor the work.

Continuity and Transformation

Working with stones cyclically builds continuity. It teaches the body and spirit to recognize rhythm. The repetition of placing, tending, cleansing, and rotating stones creates a subtle structure that supports transformation.

Transformation rarely happens all at once. It unfolds through phases. Stones remind us of this. They hold steady while change moves around them. They anchor intention through the turning of days and seasons. They demonstrate that growth does not require constant motion. It requires consistency.

As you dedicate stones to cycles, you deepen your relationship with time itself. You begin to notice patterns. You feel when something is waxing or waning. You become attuned not only to external seasons, but to your own internal tides.

And in that awareness, magic becomes less about forcing outcomes and more about aligning with rhythm.
The stone remains. The seasons turn. You change.
And through it all, the Earthbound Allies hold steady.

Anchoring the Turning of the Wheel

The Wheel turns whether we notice it or not.
Solstices, equinoxes, and the cross-quarter days mark subtle and powerful shifts in light, temperature, growth, decay, and renewal. By rotating stones on your altar in alignment with these seasonal thresholds, you create continuity between the Earth's movement and your own inner transformation.

This practice does not require elaborate ceremony. It requires attention. At each seasonal turning, pause. Remove the stones that have been holding the previous season's energy. Cleanse them gently. Thank them for their work. Then place new stones aligned with the incoming current of the Wheel.

Over time, this ritual becomes a steady rhythm that grounds your practice in lived experience rather than abstraction. Below is a simple guide to support your seasonal rotation.

Pairing Stones with Herbs

When stones and herbs are aligned, they support and stabilize each other. Herbs move. They release aroma, infuse water, rise in smoke, and interact quickly with body and breath. Stones remain steady. They anchor, contain, and hold frequency over time. Together, they create a balanced current of motion and stability, expansion and containment. One carries intention outward. The other roots it deeply.

Pairing stones with herbs is an act of energetic layering. The plant offers immediacy and responsiveness. The stone offers endurance and structure. When blended thoughtfully, the qualities of each reinforce the other. A tea sipped beside a dedicated crystal. A sachet resting atop a grounding stone. An altar bowl combining petals and polished mineral. These combinations weave subtle forces into a unified field.

Some harmonious pairings include:

- **Rose quartz with rose, hibiscus, or lavender** for love, compassion, and heart healing. The softness of the herbs opens emotional flow, while rose quartz steadies and sustains that openness.
- **Black tourmaline with rosemary or sage** for protection and clearing. The herbs cleanse and refresh the energetic field, while tourmaline anchors boundaries and absorbs excess.
- **Citrine with cinnamon, bay, or mint** for abundance and manifestation. The herbs stimulate momentum and intention, while citrine amplifies confidence and sustained focus.
- **Moonstone with mugwort or jasmine** for intuition and dreamwork. The herbs enhance receptivity and symbolic awareness, while moonstone stabilizes emotional tides.
- **Smoky quartz with patchouli or vetiver** for grounding and embodiment. The earthy scent anchors the senses, while smoky quartz draws scattered energy back into the body.

These pairings can be worked with in many forms. Place a crystal beside your tea cup as it steeps. Rest a stone atop a jar of dried herbs dedicated to a specific purpose. Carry a small herb sachet alongside a tumbled stone in your pocket. The method matters less than the presence you bring to it. When intention is clear, the partnership forms naturally.

Let intuition guide combinations. Energetic harmony matters more than rigid correspondence charts. Notice how the pairing feels in your hand, in your breath, in your awareness. Does the energy feel balanced or overwhelming? Calm or scattered? Your body is an instrument for sensing alignment. Trust its signals.

Over time, you may find certain stone and herb partnerships become personal allies, carrying layered meaning from repeated ritual. They begin to feel familiar, like trusted companions. In this way, pairing stones with herbs becomes less about theory and more about relationship. You are not merely combining materials. You are weaving breath and bone, root and crystal, into living magic grounded in both movement and permanence.

Ethical Considerations and Respect
Stones deserve ethical consideration. Many are mined under difficult conditions, and not all sources are sustainable.

When possible:
- Purchase from transparent sellers
- Choose locally found stones
- Work deeply with fewer stones rather than collecting excessively

Magic rooted in respect carries greater integrity and strength.

Reflection & Journaling Prompts

Which stone are you currently most drawn to, and what might that attraction be revealing about your present season of life?

____

____

____

____

When you sit quietly with a stone, what sensations arise in your body?

____

____

____

____

____

If one of your stones could speak, what would it say about the intention you have been asking it to hold?

____

____

____

____

____

____

Reflection & Journaling Prompts

What patterns do you notice in the types of stones you are drawn to?

____

____

____

____

____

____

____

____

How do you currently care for your stone allies, and where might you deepen that relationship?

____

____

____

____

____

____

____

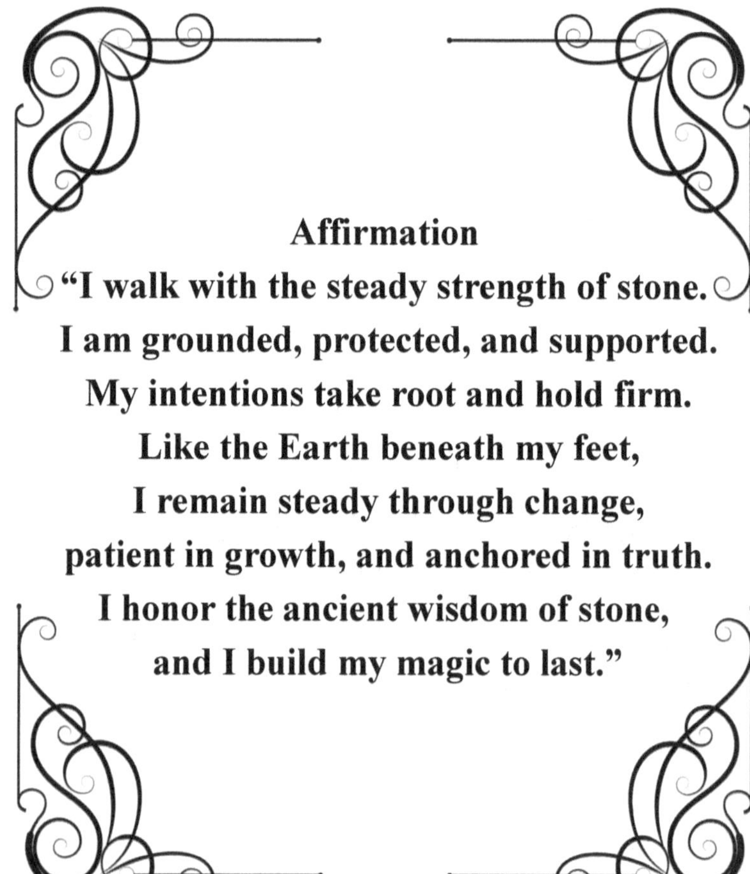

Affirmation

"I walk with the steady strength of stone.
I am grounded, protected, and supported.
My intentions take root and hold firm.
Like the Earth beneath my feet,
I remain steady through change,
patient in growth, and anchored in truth.
I honor the ancient wisdom of stone,
and I build my magic to last."

The Path Home

You have completed the circle, dear one. The flame of transformation burns steady within you now, no longer wild and searching, but focused, patient, and bright. What once flickered with uncertainty now glows with quiet confidence. The herbs know your touch. The Elements recognize your presence. The Moon knows your rhythm and meets you as an old friend.

You began this journey seeking knowledge, collecting correspondences, learning names, memorizing rituals. Yet what unfolded was far deeper than information. You discovered relationship. You learned to listen instead of control, to align instead of force. In the tending of roots and resins, in the watching of cycles and phases, you remembered something ancient within yourself. You are no longer separate from the magic you practice. You have become its living expression.

The path has not made you perfect. It has made you present. It has taught you to sit with shadow without fear, to welcome growth without impatience, to release without clinging. You have learned that power does not shout. It steadies. It roots. It breathes. This steadiness is the true gold of your work.

Take a breath now. Feel the pulse of the Earth beneath your feet and the hum of the stars above. Notice how your body stands between them, grounded and reaching all at once. You are the bridge. You are the meeting point of soil and sky, matter and spirit. Through you, Heaven touches Earth. Through you, intention becomes form.

The Wheel will continue to turn. There will be winters that ask for rest, springs that demand courage, summers that test your vitality, and autumns that require release. But you no longer fear the turning. You know how to move with it. You trust the rhythm because you have lived it.

Close this grimoire not as an ending, but as a beginning. Not as a final page, but as a doorway. The true work does not live in ink. It lives in your breath, your garden, your kitchen, your quiet moments of choice. It lives in how you tend your life with awareness and reverence.

Return to yourself often. Touch soil. Brew tea. Watch the Moon. Light a candle when you forget and need remembering. The path home is not somewhere distant. It is the steady center within you that has been guiding you all along.

Now, root to sky, may your light rise.
May your hands bless what they touch.
May your presence soften what feels hard.
May your fire remain warm and unwavering.
The witch's journey never ends. It only deepens.

Root to Sky:
A Witch's Farewell &
Benediction for the Path Ahead

"Rooted in Earth, reaching toward Light, I am the circle made whole."

The Final Whisper
Dear one, you have walked the spiral path, through shadow and sun, seed and bloom, root and ritual.

You have listened to the voice of the Earth, danced beneath the Moon, and remembered what your soul always knew: You are not separate from nature; you are nature, dreaming itself awake.

The herbs have spoken to you in scent and song.
The Elements have walked beside you in wind, flame, wave, and soil.
The Moon has kept her rhythm as your mirror and guide.

Now, as you close this book, know that the journey does not end; it simply deepens.
The Green Path continues in every breath you take, every tea you brew, every seed you plant with love.
Magic is not only found in ritual; it is found in the living.

The Witch's Benediction
May your roots sink deep into fertile soil,
anchored in gratitude and grace.
May your branches reach boldly toward the Sun,
unafraid to bloom in your own divine timing.
May your heart stay soft as moss and strong as oak,
open to both mystery and truth.
May your hands remember how to heal,
and your spirit remembers how to rest.
May you walk gently upon this Earth,
leaving blessings with every step.
And when you look up at the Moon,
May she whisper back:
"You are magic, beloved. You always have been."

A Parting Spell of Light
"Earth beneath me, steady and kind.
Fire within me, radiant mind.
Water around me, flow and renew.
Air above me, clear and true.
Spirit within me, whole and free.
Root to Sky, I am all that I need."

So it is.
So it was.
So it shall ever be.
Blessed Be, always.
 Holly Fitzpatrick

Additional Rituals

The Soil Memory Ritual

Purpose: Grounding, belonging, nervous system calm

Element: Earth

Planetary Influence: Saturn (stability, boundaries), Earth

Best Timing: Waning Moon, early morning

Ritual:

Hold a small bowl of soil gathered respectfully from your land or a place of safety.

Press your hands into the soil and breathe deeply.

Speak aloud what you wish to release or steady.

When finished, return the soil to the Earth or a living plant as an offering.

Whisper:

"I am held. I am rooted. I belong."

Notes:

Use during times of transition, grief, or overwhelm.

Create your own

Name:

Purpose:

Element:

Planetary Influence:

Best Timing:

Ritual:

The Green Thread Blessing

Purpose: Gentle protection, energetic harmony

Element: Earth + Air

Planetary Influence: Venus (harmony), Saturn (protection)

Best Timing: Waxing Moon, Friday

Ritual:

Tie a length of green thread around a plant stem, garden stake, or door handle.

As you knot the thread, visualize protection forming softly rather than forcefully.

Leave until it naturally fades or breaks, then bury it.

Whisper:

"Bound in care, released in trust."

Notes:

Ideal for home, garden, or personal energetic boundaries.

Create your own

Name:

Purpose:

Element:

Planetary Influence:

Best Timing:

Ritual:

The Breath of Leaves Spell

Purpose: Mental clarity, focus, emotional lightness

Element: Air

Planetary Influence: Mercury (clarity, communication)

Best Timing: Waxing Moon, Wednesday

Ritual:

Sit near a tree or houseplant.

Inhale while brushing fingers gently over leaves.

Exhale, imagining thoughts dispersing like mist.

Continue until breath and mind slow.

Whisper:

"My thoughts clear as the open sky."

Notes:

Excellent before writing, study, or decision-making.

Create your own

Name:

Purpose:

Element:

Planetary Influence:

Best Timing:

Ritual:

The Morning Water Rite

Purpose: Daily alignment, energetic reset

Element: Water

Planetary Influence: Moon (intuition), Sun (vitality)

Best Timing: Sunrise

Ritual:

Hold a glass of water near sunlight.

Add one fresh herb or leaf.

Speak gratitude for the coming day and drink slowly.

Whisper:

"I begin in harmony."

Notes:

May be practiced daily without depletion.

Create your own

Name:

Purpose:

Element:

Planetary Influence:

Best Timing:

Ritual:

The Root Release Ritual

Purpose: Letting go, emotional composting

Element: Earth

Planetary Influence: Pluto (transformation), Saturn (closure)

Best Timing: Waning or Dark Moon

Ritual:

Write what you are ready to release.

Bury the paper beneath soil or roots.

Water lightly and walk away.

Whisper:

"What ends nourishes what begins."

Notes:

Do not revisit the buried intention.

Create your own

Name:

Purpose:

Element:

Planetary Influence:

Best Timing:

Ritual:

The Plant Ally Listening Ritual

Purpose: Intuition, guidance, relationship-building

Element: Earth + Spirit

Planetary Influence: Moon (intuition), Mercury (messages)

Best Timing: Any Moon phase

Ritual:

Sit with a single plant.

Place your hand nearby without touching.

Ask what lesson it offers.

Listen quietly, then record impressions.

Whisper:

 "I listen with respect."

Notes:

Responses may arrive later through dreams or insight.

Create your own

Name:

Purpose:

Element:

Planetary Influence:

Best Timing:

Ritual:

The Hearth Renewal Spell

Purpose: Home harmony, emotional warmth

Element: Fire + Water

Planetary Influence: Sun (vitality), Venus (comfort)

Best Timing: Full Moon or Sunday

Ritual:

Simmer rosemary, citrus peel, and salt.

Let steam rise through your home as you move slowly through each room.

Whisper:

"This space is warmed with peace."

Notes:

Particularly powerful after conflict or illness.

Create your own

Name:

Purpose:

Element:

Planetary Influence:

Best Timing:

Ritual:

The Moonless Garden Blessing

Purpose: Private intentions, subtle manifestation

Element: Earth + Void

Planetary Influence: Dark Moon, Pluto

Best Timing: Dark Moon

Ritual:

Stand quietly near soil.

Place hands over the Earth and silently name one intention.

Leave without speaking aloud.

Notes:

For desires that require protection and time.

Create your own

Name:

Purpose:

Element:

Planetary Influence:

Best Timing:

Ritual:

The Green Witch Hands Rite

Purpose: Preparation for healing or craft

Element: Earth + Water

Planetary Influence: Moon (healing), Mercury (skill)

Best Timing: Full Moon or harvest season

Ritual:

Scatter birdseed, herbs, or compostable offerings while naming gratitude. Walk away without looking back.

Whisper:

 "What I give returns in blessing."

Notes:

Never perform from a place of lack.

Create your own

Name:

Purpose:

Element:

Planetary Influence:

Best Timing:

Ritual:

The Gratitude Scatter Spell

Purpose: Sustained abundance, reciprocity

Element: Earth + Air

Planetary Influence: Jupiter (abundance), Venus (generosity)

Best Timing: Before herbal or magical work

Ritual:

Wash hands with warm, herb-infused water.

Dry slowly, focusing on intention.

Whisper:

 "These hands work in harmony with life."

Notes:

Repeat as needed to reset energy.

Create your own

Name:

Purpose:

Element:

Planetary Influence:

Best Timing:

Ritual:

Appendix
Planetary & Elemental Reference Tables

This appendix serves as a quick reference for aligning your herbal practice with planetary forces, elemental energies, and lunar timing. Use these correspondences to deepen your rituals, refine your blends, and harmonize your work with natural and cosmic rhythms. Remember, correspondences are guides, not rigid laws. Trust your intuition first. The plants will always speak.

Planetary Correspondence Table

Element	Core Energy	Magical Focus	Herbal Types	Sample Herbs
Earth	Stability, grounding protection	Security, prosperity, endurance	Roots, bark, resins	Dandelion root, Patchouli, Cedar, Oak
Air	Clarity, intellect, inspire	Communication, insight, divination	Leaves, aromatic herbs	Lavender, Peppermint, Thyme
Fire	Action, transformv itality	Manifest courage, purification	Spices, warming herbs	Cinnamon, Ginger, Basil
Water	Emotion, intuition, healing	Love, dreams, spiritual connection	Flowers, soothing herbs	Rose, Chamomile, Mugwort

Balancing Elements in Blends

For a balanced blend, consider combining:
One grounding Earth herb
One activating Fire or Air herb
One harmonizing Water herb
This creates synergy between body, mind, and spirit.

Moon Phase	Magical Focus	Best Herbal Work
New Moon	Intention setting, beginnings	Plant seeds, start new tinctures
Waxing Moon	Growth, attraction	Prosperity blends, confidence elixirs
Full Moon	Empowerment, amplification	Charge oils, finalize spellwork
Waning Moon	Release, banishing	Detox teas, protection blends
Dark Moon	Deep shadow work	Cleansing rituals, ancestral healing

Quick Alignment Guide

If your intention is:
Love → Venus + Water + Full Moon
Protection → Mars or Saturn + Earth + Waning Moon
Abundance → Jupiter + Earth + Waxing Moon
Clarity → Mercury + Air + Waxing Moon
Healing → Moon + Water + Full Moon
Layering these correspondences turns simple herbal work into advanced alchemical practice.

A Final Note on Correspondences

These tables are maps, not rules. The most powerful magic happens when knowledge meets intuition.
If a Fire herb feels like Water to you in a particular moment, listen. Your relationship with the plant matters more than tradition alone.
The Earth does not demand perfection. She asks only presence.

Appendix II
Crystal Correspondence Table

Earthbound Allies: Stones, Planets & Elements

Crystals, like herbs, carry vibrational signatures shaped by Earth and cosmos. When paired consciously with plants, lunar timing, and planetary energy, they deepen and anchor your magical work.

Use this table as a reference when creating rituals, elixirs, altar layouts, or layered spellwork.

Remember, correspondences are guides. Your intuitive relationship with a stone is always the most powerful alignment.

Elemental Crystal Correspondence Table

Element	Core Energy	Magical Focus	Crystals
Earth	Grounding, stability, protection	Security, prosperity, endurance	Hematite, Jasper, Obsidian, Smoky Quartz
Air	Clarity, communication, inspiration	Insight, intuition, expression	Clear Quartz, Fluorite, Celestite
Fire	Passion, vitality, transformation	Courage, manifestation, power	Carnelian, Garnet, Sunstone
Water	Emotion, intuition, healing	Love, dreams, psychic awareness	Moonstone, Amethyst, Aquamarine

Planetary Crystal Correspondence Table

Planet	Energy & Focus	Sample Crystals
Sun	Confidence, vitality, success	Sunstone, Citrine, Tiger's
Moon	Intuition, dreams, emotional	Moonstone, Selenite, Pearl
Mercury	Communication, intellect	Fluorite, Agate, Clear Quartz
Venus	Love, beauty, harmony	Rose Quartz, Emerald,
Mars	Action, courage, protection	Carnelian, Bloodstone, Red
Jupiter	Growth, abundance,	Lapis Lazuli, Amethyst, Green
Saturn	Boundaries, discipline,	Onyx, Hematite, Smoky Quartz

Lunar Phase Crystal Alignment

Moon Phase	Crystal Focus	Suggested Stones
New Moon	Intention setting	Clear Quartz, Moonstone
Waxing Moon	Attraction & growth	Green Aventurine,
Full Moon	Amplification & charging	Selenite, Clear Quartz, Amethyst
Waning Moon	Release & protection	Obsidian, Smoky Quartz
Dark Moon	Shadow work	Black Tourmaline,

Pairing Crystals with Herbs

For advanced layering in ritual work:
Love Work:
Rose + Rose Quartz + Venus Day

Protection:
Rosemary + Black Tourmaline + Waning Moon

Abundance:
Basil + Citrine + Thursday

Dream Work:
Mugwort + Amethyst + Full Moon

Grounding After Ritual: Patchouli + Hematite + Saturn Day

When pairing, hold both the herb and stone in your hands and feel the energetic harmony. If the vibration feels calm and unified, the pairing is aligned.

Working with Stones in Herbal Alchemy

You may:
• Place crystals near jars while tinctures steep
• Surround elixirs with a crystal grid during charging
• Store corresponding stones with herbal sachets
• Hold stones during ritual tea ceremonies
• Create altar pairings of herb bundle and stone
Always cleanse stones between uses, especially after protection or shadow work.

Ethical & Energetic Considerations

Just as with herbs, crystals deserve respect.
• Source from ethical, transparent suppliers
• Avoid stones mined through exploitative labor practices
• Cleanse stones gently using smoke, moonlight, or sound
• Remember that crystals amplify energy, so your intention matters
The Earth offers both leaf and stone as allies. Work with them as companions, not commodities.

Quick Alignment Guide

If your intention is:
Love → Rose Quartz + Venus + Water

Protection → Black Tourmaline + Saturn + Earth

Abundance → Citrine + Jupiter + Fire

Intuition → Amethyst + Moon + Water

Confidence → Sunstone + Sun + Fire

Layer crystal, herb, planet, and moon phase for full-spectrum magical resonance.

Appendix III
Herbal Safety, Contraindications & Responsible Practice

Herbs are powerful allies. They nourish, soothe, strengthen, and restore. Yet like all forms of medicine, plant medicine deserves respect, knowledge, and responsibility.

The information contained in this book is provided for educational, informational, and spiritual purposes only. It is not intended as medical advice and should not be used as a substitute for consultation with a qualified healthcare professional.

The author is not a licensed physician, medical practitioner, or clinical herbalist. The reader assumes full responsibility for how the information in this book is interpreted and applied.

Always consult a qualified healthcare provider before using herbs, supplements, essential oils, or alternative practices, especially if you are pregnant, nursing, taking medication, managing a health condition, or administering herbs to children or elderly individuals.

Your safety is sacred. Your body is wise. When in doubt, pause and seek guidance.

General Herbal Safety Guidelines

• Begin with small amounts when trying a new herb.

• Introduce one new herb at a time to monitor reactions.

• Properly identify wild plants before harvesting. When in doubt, do not ingest.

• Store dried herbs in airtight containers away from heat and light.

• Label all preparations with ingredients and dates.

• Keep herbal preparations out of reach of children and pets. Individual responses to herbs vary. Natural substances may cause allergic reactions, digestive discomfort, skin irritation, or interactions with medications.

Pregnancy & Nursing Precautions

Certain herbs discussed in this book may not be appropriate during pregnancy or breastfeeding. Some plants may influence hormonal balance or uterine activity.

Herbs traditionally contraindicated during pregnancy include, but are not limited to:

• Mugwort

• Wormwood

• Pennyroyal

• Blue Cohosh

• Black Cohosh

• High doses of Sage

• Yarrow in medicinal quantities

Always consult a qualified healthcare professional before using herbal preparations during pregnancy or while nursing.

Medication Interactions

Some herbs may interact with prescription or over-the-counter medications, including:

• Antidepressants

• Blood pressure medications

• Blood thinners

• Diabetes medications

• Hormonal therapies

• Sedatives

Examples include: St. John's Wort, which may alter the effectiveness of numerous medications

• Ginkgo, garlic, and ginger in medicinal doses, which may affect clotting

• Licorice root, which may influence blood pressure

• Ginseng, which may affect blood sugar

Consult a healthcare provider before combining herbs with any medication.

Essential Oil Safety

Essential oils are highly concentrated plant extracts and must be used responsibly.

• Do not ingest essential oils unless supervised by a qualified professional.

• Always dilute essential oils in a carrier oil before applying to the skin.

• Perform a patch test before widespread use.

• Avoid use during pregnancy unless approved by a healthcare provider.

• Use caution around pets and children.

Improper use may result in burns, irritation, toxicity, or adverse reactions.

Foraging & Identification Responsibility

The reader assumes full responsibility for correct plant identification. Misidentification of wild plants can result in serious illness or harm.

Never harvest plants unless you are completely certain of their identity.

Avoid harvesting near roadways, contaminated soil, or pesticide-treated areas.

Follow the one-third rule when harvesting, never take more than one-third of a plant population. Avoid endangered or protected species.

The author and publisher are not responsible for adverse outcomes resulting from improper identification or preparation.

Allergy & Sensitivity Notice

Individuals with plant allergies, particularly those sensitive to members of the Asteraceae family, should exercise caution with herbs such as chamomile or calendula.

Discontinue use immediately if any adverse reaction occurs.

Seek medical attention for severe symptoms including difficulty breathing, swelling, or persistent discomfort.

Spiritual & Energetic Practice

Magical and spiritual practices described in this book are shared as traditional and personal practices. Results vary by individual.

Ground yourself after deep ritual work. Rest and hydrate after emotional or energetic practices. Do not engage in intense spiritual work while exhausted or emotionally unstable.

Spiritual wellness and physical wellness are intertwined.

Limitation of Liability

By reading and applying the information in this book, the reader acknowledges that all practices are undertaken voluntarily and at their own risk.

The author and publisher disclaim liability for any direct or indirect damages arising from the use, misuse, or application of the information contained herein.

Herbalism and spiritual practice require discernment, education, and care. Seek professional medical assistance for serious or persistent health concerns.

A Final Word

The Green Witch walks gently with the Earth, honoring both mystery and responsibility.

May your practice be empowered by wisdom.

May your healing be guided by discernment.

May your magic be rooted in care.

About the Author

Helping You Create the Life You Truly Desire

Holly Fitzpatrick is an intuitive guide, Integrated Healing Arts Practitioner, and the founder of Authentic Self Revealed, a soul-centered sanctuary devoted to helping women create lives of less stress and more joy.

Her work weaves together life and mindset coaching, energy healing, hypnotherapy, lived experience, and divine intuitive gifts to support deep, sustainable transformation. Holly specializes in working with women who feel stressed, overwhelmed, and frustrated, especially empaths and highly sensitive people who often carry more than their share of emotional and energetic weight.

Rather than offering a one-size-fits-all solution, Holly creates personalized, holistic plans designed to gently release perceived blocks and barriers while honoring each individual's needs, rhythm, and inner wisdom. She is known for holding safe and sacred spaces where clients feel seen, supported, and empowered to explore their true desires without judgment.

Holly's mission is rooted in integrity, compassion, and empowerment. She guides women through stress management, pain management, and life transitions, helping them develop both practical tools and spiritual practices that lead to greater fulfillment, confidence, and joy. Her approach is both grounded and intuitive, blending modern psychology with ancient wisdom to create real-world change.

Beyond her one-on-one work, Holly is also a modern-day Green Witch, writer, and creator. Through her thoughtfully crafted workbooks, journals, books, and ritual tools, as well as her hand-blended lotions and potions, she offers tangible ways for others to bring healing, intention, and magic into everyday life. Each creation is designed to support self-discovery, nervous system regulation, emotional balance, and soulful ritual, bridging the gap between inner work and daily practice.

At the heart of everything Holly does is the belief that magic is not something external or exclusive. It is a natural state of being that emerges when we reconnect with ourselves, the Earth, and the wisdom we already carry within.

Connect & Discover More:

AuthenticSelfRevealed.com

authenticselfrevealed.com/shop

authenticholly@gmail.com

Etsy shop:
etsy.com/shop/LessStressMoreJoy

Amazon author page:
amazon.com/author/hollyfitzpatrick

Facebook:
facebook.com/authentichollyfitzpatrick